P9-BXW-076

Other books in The New York Public Library Book of Answers
Series

The Book of Answers by Barbara Berliner with Melinda Corey and
George Ochoa

Movies and TV: The New York Public Library Book of Answers by
Melinda Corey and George Ochoa

Literature: The New York Public Library Book of Answers by Melinda
Corey and George Ochoa

A Stonesong Press Book

A Fireside Book

Published by Simon & Schuster

New York ▦ London ▦ Toronto
Sydney ▦ Tokyo ▦ Singapore

AMERICAN HISTORY:

The New York Public Library Book of Answers

Melinda Corey
and
George Ochoa

FIRESIDE
Rockefeller Center
1230 Avenue of the Americas
New York, New York 10020

Copyright © 1993 by The New York Public Library
and The Stonesong Press, Inc.
A Stonesong Press Book

All rights reserved
including the right of reproduction
in whole or in part in any form.

FIRESIDE and colophon are registered trademarks
of Simon & Schuster Inc.

Designed by Mary Sarah Quinn
Manufactured in the United States of America

10 9 8 7 6 5 4 3 2 1

Library of Congress Cataloging-in-Publication Data is available.

ISBN: 0-671-79634-8

The name "The New York Public Library" and the representation of the lion
appearing in this Work are trademarks and the property of The New York
Public Library, Astor, Lenox and Tilden Foundations.

To the memory of Rudolph Burghauser,
who thought our books were "super"

—M.C. and G.O.

Acknowledgments

As usual, this book would not have been possible without the people who helped to see it to completion. We thank Paul Fargis and Gail Winston for their support throughout the project, and Tom Brown for his keyboarding of the manuscript.

Contents

Introduction

The fourth book in the New York Public Library Book of Answers series focuses on the subject many Americans like best—their own story. People like to look at themselves, and 250 million Americans have many ways to do so. A favorite method of satisfying their curiosity is to call the New York Public Library Telephone Reference Service (TelRef). At any given moment, librarians in the TelRef room may field questions ranging from "Where is Okefenokee Swamp?" to "Who was Jim Crow?" to "How old is the CIA?" along with several requests for the names of the faces on Mount Rushmore.

As always, our questions have been inspired by the types of information that callers seek from TelRef and throughout the New York Public Library reference system. Many of the questions are quirky (Who was the "Gerry" behind gerrymandering?), many serious (How many internment camps were built to house Japanese-Americans during World War II?), some traditional (Who is buried in Grant's tomb?), some with a humorous twist (What was the first name of the federal official named Nixon whom the U.S. Senate impeached?). All are the kinds of things people actually want to know.

Over the course of writing four *Books of Answers,* we have developed some guiding principles. First and foremost, we follow our subtitle and ask "unusual and entertaining questions." This has been a goal for the entire series, beginning with the original, *The Book of Answers,* which explored the whole range of knowledge, from The Animal World to Who Was Who. It has continued through the sequels: *Movies and TV, Literature,* and now, *American History.*

In addition to taking an offbeat approach to our subjects, we also aim to be representative. To that end, we have divided *American History* into 32 chapters meant to reflect a representative view of American history as it is seen today. Not forgotten are traditional subject areas like Government and Politics, the American Revolution, and Foreign Affairs. But emphasized more than we remember in our own schooling are the lives of everyday people, in chapters like Coming to America, Popular Culture, and Everyday Life. Chapters on Native American, African-American, women's, and labor history also reflect a modern concern that American history encompass the stories of all of its citizens. We also have tried to be more inclusive geographically than even the Miss America Pageant, which, as one of our answers reveals, has represented only 27 states among its 70 winners.

Because we too are human, some subjects are more equal than others. We devote chapters to them because they, in addition to being worthy, reflect areas of personal interest. For one of us, a former volunteer at the New York Catholic Worker house founded by Dorothy Day, it is the chapter on Reformers and Radicals. For another, the child of a World War II tail gunner in the Army Air Corps who spent nine months in a German prisoner-of-war camp, it is the chapter on World War II.

Likewise, there are differences in the kinds of questions to which each of us is drawn. While both of us tend toward the offbeat, one of us is more concerned with the international context of American history, while the other is devoted to domestic affairs. The result is that one of us prefers questions like, "Did Sigmund Freud ever visit the U.S.?" while the other asks, "At the 1939 New York World's Fair, how large were the Trylon and the Perisphere?"

Both of us agree on brevity. Following in the tradition of the TelRef system, which provides answers only to questions that require less than five minutes of research, we have kept our answers succinct. However, our research time on this book has often far exceeded the NYPL time limit. Issues brought up by seemingly simple questions led us to hours of related research. The question "When did Superman die?" led one of us to read a history of American comics and run out on a rainy afternoon to purchase *Superman* No. 75 (complete with black armband). A question on how the Elks chose their namesake led another to track down archival notes indicating that the original choice to represent the fraternal order had been a buffalo.

Still, be it the history of the Whig Party or Levittown, *American History: The New York Public Library Book of Answers* will not provide a complete view of any subject. It will not tell all the details of Commodore Perry's visit to Japan or list every variety of tulip exhibited in the Tulip Festival in Holland, Michigan. The book does provide a factual, impressionistic history of the United States from the date of the first human migration to the Americas to the nagging question of whether the song "Louie, Louie" contains dirty lyrics.

Many authors have a purpose for their books greater than the words that appear on the page—a change of mind about an issue, a new understanding of humanity. Reference book writers are no different. Our agenda involves rousing people to pursue knowledge. Just as we, in researching the book, felt compelled to learn more about the history of Superman and the reasons behind the formation of the Elks, we hope that you will be equally spurred by one of the book's 900-odd entries. Put simply, we hope that *American History: The New York Public Library Book of Answers* raises some questions.

AMERICAN HISTORY:

The New York
Public Library
Book of Answers

African-American History

Who was the first child of African parents born in England's American colonies?
A boy named William, born in 1623 or 1624 in Jamestown, Virginia. His parents, Antony and Isabel, were among the first Africans shipped in bondage to the English colonies in 1619.

What was the name of the first slave ship built in the English colonies?
It was the *Desire,* launched from Marblehead, Massachusetts, in 1637. Until then, only European ships transported slaves to the colonies.

What was the first American colony to abolish slavery?
Vermont in 1777. The first of the original 13 Colonies to abolish slavery was Pennsylvania in 1780.

When was the importation of slaves outlawed in the U.S.?
On January 1, 1808—nearly six decades before the 13th Amendment to the Constitution abolished slavery in 1865. However, it is estimated that 54,000 additional slaves were brought illegally to the U.S. between 1808 and the Civil War.

What dispute led to the founding of the African Methodist Episcopal Church?

The origins of the A.M.E. Church lay in a controversy over segregation rules at St. George's Methodist Church in Philadelphia in 1787. The white elders ordered black members of the congregation to sit in a separate gallery. Several African-Americans, including Richard Allen, an ex-slave and lay preacher, refused, founding their own Methodist congregation, the Bethel Church. In 1816, Allen went further, founding the A.M.E. Church, the first independent, black-run Protestant denomination. The A.M.E. church became active in philanthropy, education, and the abolitionist movement.

What was the first black newspaper?
Freedom's Journal, which began publication in New York City on March 16, 1827. Co-founders Samuel E. Cornish and John B. Russwurm explained in their first issue, "We wish to plead our own cause. Too long have others spoken for us."

How big was the price on Harriet Tubman's head?
The reward for the capture of Tubman (c. 1820–1913), an ex-slave who became famous for helping southern slaves escape to freedom in Canada, went as high as $40,000. Even so, she eluded bounty hunters, returning 19 times to the South and bringing over 300 slaves to freedom on what was called the Underground Railroad. Tubman also served as a Union nurse, scout, and spy in the Civil War.

Where in the South was Sojourner Truth (c. 1797–1883) born?
Though born into slavery, Truth was born not in the South but in Ulster County, New York, before slavery was abolished in that state in 1827. After being sold to a master who set her free, she worked as a domestic. She later became a preacher of Christianity, abolitionism, and women's rights.

Where did Frederick Douglass get his last name?

After escaping from slavery in 1838, the abolitionist and black leader (c. 1817–95) took the name "Douglass" from a character in Sir Walter Scott's narrative poem *The Lady of the Lake* (1810).

At its height, what was the slave population in the U.S.?
In the year 1860, on the eve of the Civil War, the slave population was 3,953,760.

What percentage of Southern families owned large plantations?
According to the 1860 census, only 4 percent of the white population of the South owned plantations large enough to be farmed by 20 or more slaves. About 1 percent owned plantations needing 50 or more slaves. Seventy-five percent of white families owned no slaves.

What does "Ku Klux Klan" mean?
Founded as a secret social fraternity in Pulaski, Tennessee, about 1866, the Klan took the first two syllables of its name from the Greek "kuklos," meaning circle. Through intimidation, terror, and violence, the ex-Confederates who founded the Ku Klux Klan sought to keep African-Americans in a subservient position.

How many Ku Klux Klan movements have there been?
The white supremacy movement has had at least three major incarnations: the first during Reconstruction (1860s–1870s), the second before and after World War I (1915–1920s; final disbandment in 1944), and the third since World War II (1946–present).

Who were the principals in the Supreme Court case, *Plessy v. Ferguson*?
In the 1896 decision that established the grounds for "separate but equal" public facilities, Homer Plessy was an octoroon (mixed race) who was arrested in Louisiana when he sat in a "white" car

on a train. John H. Ferguson was the New Orleans criminal court judge who convicted him.

Who wrote "Of Mr. Booker T. Washington and Others"?

W. E. B. Du Bois in *The Souls of Black Folk* (1903). Du Bois took issue with Washington's idea that blacks had to prove their worth to whites. Du Bois encouraged blacks to take pride in their African origins and to struggle for political, educational, and economic justice.

Who was the first president to invite an African-American man to the White House?

Theodore Roosevelt, who invited Booker T. Washington.

What event sparked the founding of the National Association for the Advancement of Colored People?

A 1908 race riot in Springfield, Massachusetts, reported by liberal New York journalist W.E. Walling inspired him to help found a national organization to speak out on behalf of equality for African-Americans. After a meeting with other concerned citizens in his apartment, including social worker Mary W. Ovington, the NAACP was organized in 1909. Its only black officer was W.E.B. Du Bois, who served as the first editor of its magazine, the *Crisis*.

When was the first "Negro History Week"?

The first "Negro History Week" was organized in the second week of February, 1926, by Carter G. Woodson. It was meant to include the birthday of Abraham Lincoln and the traditional birthday of Frederick Douglass. It was expanded in the 1960s to "Black History Month."

Who popularized the slogan "Africa for the Africans at home and abroad"?

The slogan was made famous by Jamaica-born black nationalist leader Marcus Garvey (1887–1940), who came to New York in

1916. Garvey built a mass movement calling for an end to op-
pression of blacks in Africa and the United States. Convicted of
mail fraud (a charge he denied), he was deported to his native
Jamaica in 1927. He died in London.

What was Elijah Muhammad's name at birth?
The leader of the Nation of Islam was born Elijah Poole in 1897
near Sandersville, Georgia. He took over leadership of the Muslim
sect (founded in Detroit in 1930 and commonly known as the
Black Muslims) in 1934, expanding its reach and advocating
black separatism until his death in 1975.

How did Jackie Robinson do in his first major league game?
The first African-American to play in the major leagues, Robinson
had no hits in three at-bats in his first game on April 15, 1947.
Playing for the Brooklyn Dodgers at Brooklyn's Ebbets Field,
Robinson fielded 11 balls in the 5–3 win against the Boston
Braves. That season, Robinson maintained a .297 average and was
named Rookie of the Year. Robinson played second base for the
Dodgers from 1947 to 1956 and was inducted into the Baseball
Hall of Fame in 1962.

For what did Ralph Bunche win the Nobel Peace Prize?
The first black to win the prize, the American statesman and civil
rights leader earned the honor in 1950 for mediating an end to
the Arab–Israeli conflict in 1949.

**Why did Rosa Parks refuse to move from her seat in the white
section of a bus in Montgomery, Alabama?**
Because of a combination of fatigue and principle. "I was quite
tired after spending a full day working," the seamstress explained
about her action on Dec. 1, 1955, which touched off the famous
bus boycott and ushered in the modern civil rights movement. In
addition, Parks was already active in the NAACP and had decided
to stand up to segregation. As she put it, the question in her mind

was "when and how would we ever determine our rights as human beings?"

Where did Dr. Martin Luther King, Jr., get his doctorate?
Born in Atlanta, King (1929–68) traveled north to receive his Ph.D. in theology from Boston University in 1955. He returned to the South to become pastor of the Dexter Avenue Baptist Church in Montgomery, Alabama, where he met Rosa Parks and was chosen to lead the bus boycott. An advocate of nonviolent protest, King went on to co-found the Southern Christian Leadership Conference (SCLC) in 1957 and worked until his death on behalf of civil rights for African-Americans.

When and where did Martin Luther King, Jr., make his "I Have a Dream" speech?
He delivered the address to more than 200,000 people on the mall between the Lincoln Memorial and the Washington Monument at the March on Washington on August 28, 1963.

Where was the first "sit-in" at a segregated lunch counter?
The protest was begun by four black college students at a Woolworth's lunch counter in Greensboro, North Carolina, on February 1, 1960. In the next two weeks, sit-ins spread to 15 cities across the South.

What did the "N" in SNCC stand for?
It originally stood for "nonviolent" when the Student Nonviolent Coordinating Committee was founded in April 1960 by sit-in veterans who wanted to step up the pace of nonviolent direct action for equal rights. As the 1960s wore on, SNCC leaders became frustrated with white repression of the civil rights movement and began to advocate the use of force in self-defense. In 1969, SNCC's name was changed to the Student National Coordinating Committee.

How did the 24th Amendment advance the cause of civil rights?
Ratified in January 1964, the 24th Amendment made it illegal to deny a citizen the right to vote in a federal election for failure to pay a poll tax. This device had been used by Southern states since Reconstruction to prevent blacks from voting.

What were the names of the three civil rights workers murdered by the Ku Klux Klan in 1964?
James Chaney, 21, Andrew Goodman, 21, and Michael Schwerner, 25. Goodman and Schwerner were white students from New York who had come to Mississippi to help in the "Freedom Summer" voter registration project. Chaney was a black Mississippian. In June 1964, the young men disappeared; six weeks later they were found beaten and shot to death.

For what crime did Malcolm X go to prison?
Born as Malcolm Little (1925–65), he served six years in prison for burglary, beginning at age 21. While in prison, he joined the Nation of Islam and took the Muslim name El-Hajj Malik El-Shabazz and the public name of Malcolm X. Malcolm became a vocal opponent of white racism and advocate for black rights. Personal and ideological differences led him to break with the Nation of Islam in 1963 and found the Organization of Afro-American Unity in 1964.

Where was Malcolm X killed?
He was shot dead on February 21, 1965, at the Audubon Ballroom in Harlem where he was preparing to speak. It is widely alleged that his assassins were members of the Nation of Islam.

How long did the Watts riots of 1965 last?
Six days, beginning on August 12, 1965. The riot in the largely black Watts district of Los Angeles involved up to 10,000 people. Thirty-four people—most of them black—were killed. Nearly

4,000 people were arrested. Whole blocks were burned, with nearly 1,000 buildings damaged or destroyed. Damage was estimated at over $200 million.

Who warned, "Our nation is moving toward two societies, one black, one white—separate and unequal"?

The warning appeared in the 1968 report of the National Advisory Commission on Civil Disorders, which was headed by Illinois governor Otto Kerner. President Johnson appointed Kerner to investigate the causes of over 100 ghetto riots that took place in the summer of 1967, the worst in Newark and Detroit. The Kerner report blamed police racism and repression and neglect of the economic and educational needs of African-Americans.

What justice did Thurgood Marshall replace on the Supreme Court?

President Lyndon Johnson appointed Marshall to fill the seat vacated by Thomas C. Clark, who resigned when his son, Ramsey Clark, was appointed as U.S. Attorney General. Marshall (1908–92), a noted civil rights lawyer, became the first African-American Supreme Court justice.

What was "Resurrection City"?

It was a shantytown built at the Lincoln Memorial in Washington, D.C., by participants in the Poor People's March on March 2, 1968. The marchers built Resurrection City to protest the poverty of black Americans and to call for federal aid. The shantytown was torn down after two months.

How many times did Jesse Jackson run for the U.S. presidency?

The first black candidate to launch a major presidential campaign, Jackson ran twice for the Democratic nomination, in 1984 and 1988.

What year was Martin Luther King Day first observed as a federal holiday?
It was first observed as a federal legal public holiday on January 20, 1986.

Who videotaped Rodney King's beating by Los Angeles police?
A white amateur photographer named George Holliday happened to be on hand to videotape the scene on March 3, 1991, while testing his new camcorder. The images of black motorist King being kicked and clubbed by white officers shocked the country. A year later, news of the white officers' acquittal on assault charges sparked three days of rioting in minority areas of Los Angeles, beginning on April 29, 1992.

Who was the first black woman senator?
Carol Moseley Braun (Democrat, Illinois), whose term began in 1993. The first black senator was Hiram Revels of Mississippi, who served during Reconstruction, 1870–71.

The American Revolution

Who won the first battle of the War of Independence?
The Massachusetts militiamen won the Battle of Lexington and Concord when they forced the British to retreat from Concord back to Boston. The British were trying to confiscate colonial arms from a depot at Concord. The battle, which took place on the night of April 18–19, 1775, was the first military encounter of the American Revolution (1775–83).

On what hill did the Battle of Bunker Hill take place?
It took place not on Bunker Hill but on Breed's Hill, on June 17, 1775. The opposing forces were supposed to engage on Bunker Hill, but for unknown reasons the soldiers dug in on the smaller site, about 2,000 feet away. To straighten things out for visitors, Breed's Hill was later renamed Bunker Hill.

What did John Hancock (1737–93) do to earn his place as president of the Continental Congress?
His most distinctive contribution to the rebel cause was money. Hancock was a merchant who had inherited a fortune from a smuggler uncle. He used his wealth to help finance the revolution. He is best remembered now for his flamboyant signature on the Declaration of Independence in 1776. After the war, Hancock became governor of Massachusetts.

How many grievances against the king were named in the Declaration of Independence?
The document cited 27 separate grievances against the king of Great Britain, George III. These grievances included refusing his assent to "wholesome" laws, making judges dependent on "his will alone," and bringing in foreign mercenaries to wage war on the colonies in a way "totally unworthy the head of a civilized nation."

Was Paul Revere of British descent?
The Revolutionary War patriot (1735–1818) was only 50 percent British. Revere's father was French silversmith Apollos Rivoire, a Huguenot (Protestant) refugee from persecution by the Catholic authorities in France. Revere's mother, Deborah Hitchbourn, was of English descent.

How cold was it at Valley Forge?
Overall, the winter was fairly mild in 1777–78 when George Washington and his Continental Army were encamped at this site 22 miles northwest of Philadelphia. There was heavy snow and freezing weather in Christmas week but a thaw in January. What made conditions miserable was lack of adequate food, clothing, and shelter due to negligence and mismanagement by the Continental Congress and the commissary department. It is estimated that 2,500 of 10,000 soldiers died of disease and exposure during this period.

Who was Marie Joseph Paul Yves Roch Gilbert du Motier?
He was the French nobleman better known to history as the Marquis de Lafayette (1757–1834). In 1777, at the age of 19, Lafayette came to America to volunteer in the Revolutionary War. Idealistic and adventurous, he was appointed a major-general and helped to secure military assistance from France.

What side won the following Revolutionary War battles:

Long Island, New York August 27, 1776	British
White Plains, New York October 28, 1776	British
Bennington, Vermont August 16, 1777	Americans
Monmouth, New Jersey June 28, 1778	British
Cowpens, South Carolina January 17, 1781	Americans

Who was Molly Pitcher?

She was Mary McCauley Hays, (1754–1832), heroine of the American Revolution. She earned her nickname during the Battle of Monmouth in 1778, when she fetched water for her husband and his gun crew. After her husband suffered a wound, she took over for him, helping the gun crew do its job. After the war, she was given a yearly pension of $40 by the Pennsylvania Assembly.

How many countries did the British fight during the American War of Independence?

By 1780, the British were fighting not only the United States and its ally France, but also Spain, the Netherlands, and the ruler of Mysore in India. The conflicts were not all related to American independence, but they did keep the British busy on many fronts, aiding the U.S. cause.

What became of British general Charles Cornwallis (1738–1805)?

In the U.S., Cornwallis's main claim to fame was his surrender to the Americans and French at Yorktown, Virginia, on October 19, 1781, a turning point that effectively ended the war. But Cornwallis's career of enforcing British imperial rule was far from over.

He went on to become Governor General of India (1786–94, 1805) and viceroy of Ireland (1798–1801).

Who were the American diplomats who negotiated the treaty that ended the Revolutionary War?
Benjamin Franklin, John Adams, and John Jay negotiated for the United States. The Treaty of Paris, ending the war and recognizing American independence, was signed on February 3, 1783.

Who was the last surviving signer of the Declaration of Independence?
Charles Carroll of Carrollton, Maryland. Born in 1737, he was 95 years old when he died in 1832.

The Civil War

What was the first state to secede from the Union?
It was South Carolina, which seceded on December 20, 1860, in response to the November election of Abraham Lincoln as president.

What military experience did the commanders of the opposing forces at Fort Sumter have in common?
Like many top officers in the Civil War, both men had fought on the same side in the Mexican War (1846–48). P.G.T. Beauregard was the Confederate general who gave the order to fire on Fort Sumter on April 12, 1861, at 4:30 A.M., in the first battle of the Civil War. His former comrade Robert Anderson surrendered the Union fort after withstanding bombardment for 34 hours.

What were the populations of the Union and the Confederacy?
The Union had a population of about 20,700,000. The 11 states of the Confederacy had a population of 9,100,000 including nearly 4,000,000 slaves.

What was Ulysses S. Grant doing when the Civil War broke out?

A West Point graduate, Grant (1822–85) had fallen into alcoholism and hard times after his service in the Mexican War. He was working as a clerk in his father's leather shop in Galena, Illinois, when the Civil War began. Obtaining a commission as a colonel of volunteers, a string of victories helped him rise quickly through the ranks. In 1864, Lincoln named him general-in-chief of all Union forces.

What role did West Virginia take during the Civil War?
The region was part of Virginia when that state seceded from the Union in 1861. The delegates of 40 western counties formed their own government and seceded from Virginia to join the Union side. These counties entered the Union as the state of West Virginia in 1863.

What was the single bloodiest day of the Civil War?
According to many historians, it was September 17, 1862, when General George McClellan's Union forces and Robert E. Lee's Confederate troops clashed in the Battle of Antietam. The savage struggle took place at Antietam Creek near Sharpsburg, Maryland, ending with the retreat of Lee's army into Virginia on September 18. The Union suffered over 12,000 casualties, with 2,100 men killed; the Confederates suffered over 10,000 casualties, with 2,700 men killed.

What side won the following Civil War battles:

First Bull Run, Virginia July 21, 1861	Confederacy
Shiloh, Tennessee April 6–7, 1862	Union
Second Bull Run, Virginia August 29–30, 1862	Confederacy
Antietam, Maryland September 17, 1862	Union

Federicksburg, Virginia December 13, 1862	Confederacy
Siege of Vicksburg, Mississippi May 22–July 4, 1863	Union
Gettysburg, Pennsylvania July 1–3, 1863	Union
The Wilderness, Virginia May 5–6, 1864	Union

Who was the other orator at the Gettysburg cemetery on the day Lincoln delivered his famous address?

The principal speaker at the ceremonies dedicating the military burial ground on November 19, 1863, was Edward Everett, former governor of Massachusetts and famous orator. His speech lasted about two hours; Lincoln's lasted two minutes. Everett wrote Lincoln: "I should be glad, if I could flatter myself that I came as near the central idea of the occasion, in two hours, as you did in two minutes."

In what Civil War battle did the first African-American win the Congressional Medal of Honor?

Sergeant William H. Carney won the medal for his courage in the charge of the 54th Massachusetts Volunteers on Fort Wagner in the harbor of Charleston, South Carolina, in July 1863. The charge was unsuccessful, but the regiment's bravery is commemorated by a monument at the Boston House of Commons. The black regiment was led by white officer Colonel Robert Gould Shaw, killed with many others in the fighting.

Was Stonewall Jackson killed by Union gunfire?

Confederate general Thomas "Stonewall" Jackson died of a battle wound, but it was not inflicted by a Union soldier. One of his own men accidentally shot him in the arm during the Battle of Chancellorsville, Virginia, May 1–3, 1863. Although the battle was a Confederate victory, Jackson's arm had to be amputated. The general contracted pneumonia and died on May 10.

What was Lincoln's "eye for an eye" order?
It was an order issued in 1863 during the Civil War that the Union would shoot a Confederate prisoner for every black Union prisoner shot, and would condemn a Confederate prisoner to hard labor for life for every black prisoner sold into slavery. The order was meant to deter Confederates from murdering or enslaving captured black soldiers.

Where did Sherman's March to the Sea begin and end?
The devastating march across Georgia began in the occupied city of Atlanta on November 11, 1864, and ended with the capture of Savannah on the Atlantic Ocean on December 21. Along the way, Sherman ransacked the countryside, looting, burning, and tearing up railroads.

Did Grant and Lee meet in a courthouse to discuss terms for Lee's surrender?
The two commanders-in-chief met at Appomattox Court House, but that was the name of a village in Virginia, not an actual courthouse. On April 9, 1865, Ulysses S. Grant accepted Robert E. Lee's surrender in the front parlor of a private house owned by farmer Wilmer McLean.

How many Americans died in the Civil War?
Union deaths from battle or disease totalled 364, 511. Authoritative figures for the Confederacy are not available, but most estimates range around 260,000. The total of 620,000 deaths makes this conflict the bloodiest in the nation's history—not excluding World War II, in which 405,399 Americans died.

Was Jefferson Davis wearing women's clothing when he was captured?

That was the unsubstantiated rumor that spread among Union soldiers after the president of the Confederacy was captured near Irwinville, Georgia, on May 10, 1865. Supposedly Davis had donned his wife's cloak and shawl to disguise himself from the enemy.

Coming to America

Who was the first known European to view America?
It was not Christopher Columbus or Leif Erikson. It was a Norseman named Biarni Heriulfson who first spotted North America around 985 A.D. Blown off course while sailing from Iceland to Greenland, he probably saw what is now Newfoundland, Canada.

How many ancient Norse settlements have been discovered in North America?
Only one: the remains of a colony at L'Anse aux Meadows in Newfoundland discovered by Norwegian archeologists in the 1960s. Settled in the 11th century, it may have been a staging area for explorations to the south.

What was the first American land visited by Columbus?
It was an island in the Bahamas that he named San Salvador. Historians have disagreed which island this really was: Watling Island and Samana Cay have both been suggested as possibilities. The landfall was first spotted on October 12, 1492, at about 2 A.M. by Rodrigo de Triana, the lookout on the *Pinta*.

What nationality was explorer John Cabot?
Italian. Born Giovanni Caboto in Genoa, Italy (c. 1450), he sailed under the English flag. He appears to have reached Newfound-

land in 1497, a year before Columbus reached the American mainland. Cabot was lost at sea in 1498.

When did the name "America" first appear in print?
In 1507 in *Cosmographiae Introductio* by German mapmaker Martin Waldseemüller. Waldseemüller named it in honor of explorer Amerigo Vespucci, whom he believed was the true discoverer of America. Vespucci's claims to have been the first to reach the American mainland (in 1497) and the first to realize that America was not part of Asia have long been disputed, but his name lives on in geography just the same.

What route did Europeans first take to get to the Mississippi River?
Spanish explorer Hernando de Soto became the first European to reach the Mississippi River during a treasure-hunting expedition in 1539–42. Sailing from Havana, Cuba, De Soto landed at Tampa Bay, Florida, and traveled by a meandering route through what are now Georgia, the Carolinas, Tennessee, Alabama, and Mississippi. After crossing the river and reaching what are now Arkansas and Louisiana, he died of a fever and was buried in the Mississippi River.

What is the oldest town founded in America by Europeans?
St. Augustine, Florida, which was settled by Spain in 1565.

What is the oldest surviving building of non-Indian design in the United States?
The Governor's Palace in Santa Fe, New Mexico, built by the Spanish in 1609.

What part of America did Sir Francis Drake call "New England"?
The English explorer gave the name *Nova Albion* (Latin for "New

England") to California in 1579. The place near San Francisco where he anchored is still called Drake's Bay.

What European country sent the first explorers to the region that is now New York state?

France. Italian explorer Giovanni Verrazzano, sailing for France in 1524, discovered New York Bay. In 1609, French soldier and sailor Samuel de Champlain explored what is now northern New York and claimed it for France. However, the Dutch were the first to colonize New York, beginning with Fort Orange (now Albany) in 1624 and New Amsterdam (now New York City) in 1626.

How many of the 13 English colonies were settled first by Europeans from other countries?

The four "Middle Colonies"—New York, New Jersey, Pennsylvania, Delaware—were all initially colonized by countries other than England. New York and New Jersey were settled by the Dutch, Delaware and Pennsylvania by the Swedes.

What became of the Swedish colony?

New Sweden, founded in 1638 with its base at what is now Wilmington, Delaware, was conquered by the Dutch in 1655. The British conquered the Dutch colonies in 1664.

How many people left England during the Great Migration of the 1630s?

Over 60,000 British settlers emigrated to New England, Bermuda, and the Caribbean islands, for economic, religious, or political reasons.

Where did the first Jews in the 13 Colonies settle?

They settled in the Dutch colony of New Amsterdam (New York) in 1654. Descendants of Jews forced to leave Spain and Portugal during persecutions in the late 15th century, they had settled in the Dutch colony of Recife in Brazil. When that colony was conquered by the Portuguese, the Jews fled to New Amsterdam.

For which King Louis was Louisiana named?
Louis XIV of France, who reigned from 1643 to 1715. The entire Mississippi River Valley was named Louisiana and claimed for France by Robert Cavelier, Sieur de la Salle, in 1682.

In what century did Europeans discover Alaska?
The 18th century. Vitus Bering, a Dane working for the Russians, and Alexei Chirikov discovered Alaska and the Aleutian Islands in 1741.

How long have people of Mexican descent lived in Los Angeles?
They founded the city in 1781. Mexicans remained the major population group in Los Angeles (named for Our Lady of the Angels) until the Gold Rush of 1849 brought Anglo-Americans to California in droves. By then, as a result of the Mexican War in 1846–48, California had passed from Mexican to U.S. possession.

What did the sign "NINA" in front of 19th-century factories mean?
It meant "No Irish Need Apply." It expressed native-born American prejudice against the two million Irish immigrants who arrived in the U.S. between 1830 and 1860.

What were the major ethnic groups employed in the building of the first transcontinental railroad?
The eastern branch, the Union Pacific, employed mainly Irish workers; the western branch, the Central Pacific, employed mainly Chinese workers. The two work crews met at Promontory, Utah, in May 1869, completing the transcontinental link.

When did "chutzpa" enter the American language?

The Yiddish word meaning "gall, impudence" came over from Eastern Europe with the millions of Jews who immigrated to the U.S. beginning in the 1880s. By the 1970s, the Americanized term had taken on the positive connotation of "self-confidence, courage" and had made its way into British slang as well.

How long did the Chinese Exclusion Act last?
The 1882 law, which was enacted to preserve jobs for native-born Americans, suspended Chinese immigration to the U.S. for ten years. Renewed from time to time in the 20th century, it was completely suspended in 1965.

What did it mean to travel to America in "steerage"?
For late 19th-century immigrants from Europe, it meant a passage below decks, near the ship's steering gear. The price for these uncomfortable but low-fare accommodations was about $15.

What was Fiorello La Guardia's job at Ellis Island?
The future mayor of New York City worked at the immigration center on Ellis Island as an interpreter while attending law school. The Manhattan-born son of an Austrian Jewish mother and Italian father, La Guardia (1882–1947) helped usher immigrants through the center, which served as a port of entry from 1892 to 1943.

What percentage of New Yorkers in 1930 were members of immigrant families?
Seventy-five percent of the population consisted of foreigners and their children. Italians and Eastern European Jews were the largest groups.

Are there more Chinese-Americans or Japanese-Americans?
According to the 1990 census, Americans of Chinese origin (1.6

million) outnumber those of Japanese origin (848,000) by almost two to one.

What is the national origin of most Hispanics in the U.S.?
Of the 22.4 million Hispanic-Americans counted in the 1990 census, more than 60 percent (13.5 million) are of Mexican heritage. Another 2.7 million are Puerto Rican, 1 million are Cuban, and the rest are "other." All together, Hispanics, who can be of any race, account for 9 percent of the U.S. population.

What immigrant group has the most descendants in the United States today?
More Americans (19.6 percent) report German ancestry than any other. In second place is Irish ancestry (13.1 percent) and in third place English (11 percent).

Disasters

What was the "Hurricane of Independence"?
It was a hurricane that swept from North Carolina to Nova Scotia from September 2–9, 1775, killing over 4,000 people. It received its name because it coincided with the first stages of the American War of Independence.

What was the worst marine disaster in U.S. history?
At least 1,547 people were killed when the boiler of the side-wheeler *Sultana* exploded on April 27, 1865, on the Mississippi River near Memphis, Tennessee. Many of those killed in the blaze were Union soldiers who had recently been freed from Confederate prison camps. The most unusual survival story was that of a man who used a knife to kill a live alligator that was in a wooden crate on board, then used the crate to float away.

What was the worst earthquake east of the Mississippi River?
It occurred in Charleston, South Carolina, on August 31, 1886, and registered what would have been 6.6 on the Richter scale. Sixty people were killed.

How big was the earthquake that hit San Francisco in 1906?
It is estimated to have measured 8.3 on the Richter scale. Four square miles of downtown San Francisco were destroyed and over

500 people died in the earthquake and subsequent fire on April 18–19, 1906.

What nationality was the *Lusitania*?
The 32,000-ton liner sunk by a German submarine on May 6, 1915, was British. Of the 1,200 passengers who lost their lives, 128 were Americans—a fact that aroused strong anti-German feeling in the U.S.

What disease was responsible for the most deadly epidemic in U.S. history?
Influenza. An epidemic from March to November 1918 killed over 500,000 people nationwide.

What started the fire at the Cocoanut Grove night club?
The fire that killed 491 people at the Boston night club on November 28, 1942, may have been started by a 16-year-old boy named Stanley Tomaszewski who lit a match near a palm tree while trying to replace a light bulb. However, the fire commissioner could not prove that the boy had started it, and the blaze was officially declared "of unknown origin."

Has an airplane ever crashed into the Empire State Building?
Yes. On July 28, 1945, a U.S. Army bomber crashed into the New York landmark, killing 13.

What was the first flood in the United States to cost $1 billion in damages?
The flooding of the Kansas River at Kansas City, Missouri, and Topeka and Lawrence, Kansas, in July 1951. Forty-one people were killed.

What causes Legionnaires' disease?
The acute pneumonia is caused by a bacterium of the genus *Legionella*. The disease made headlines (and got its name) when it

killed 29 people at an American Legion convention in Philadelphia, July 21–24, 1976. The causative agent was found a year later.

What were the names of the seven crew members killed when the space shuttle *Challenger* exploded?
The seven people killed in the explosion on January 28, 1986, 73 seconds after lift-off, were:

Gregory B. Jarvis
Christa McAuliffe
Ronald E. McNair
Ellison S. Onizuka
Judith A. Resnick
Francis R. Scobee
Michael J. Smith

How many gallons of oil did the *Exxon Valdez* spill into Prince William Sound?
After hitting an undersea reef, the tanker spilled over 10 million gallons into the Alaskan waters on March 24, 1989, in the worst oil spill in U.S. history.

What game of the World Series was about to begin when the San Francisco earthquake of 1989 struck?
The earthquake hit the San Francisco Bay area on October 17, 1989, minutes before the third game of the World Series was about to be played between the Oakland Athletics and the San Francisco Giants. The earthquake, which measured 7.1 on the Richter scale, killed 67 people and destroyed over 100,000 buildings.

How strong were the winds of Hurricane Andrew?
The most destructive hurricane in U.S. history, Andrew's winds reached speeds of 175 miles per hour as they gusted into Dade

County, Florida, on August 24, 1992. South-central Louisiana was hit by 120 mile-per-hour winds two days later. The hurricane killed 38 people and caused billions of dollars in losses.

How many people in the U.S. have been diagnosed with AIDS?
According to the Centers for Disease Control, about 250,000 AIDS cases have been reported in the U.S. and its territories as of September 30, 1992. Of those people, 160,372 have died.

Economic History

What was the first major export industry in America?
Tobacco. By 1617, 50,000 pounds of the Virginia-grown crop were exported to England.

What was produced at the first American factory?
Yarn. It was produced at Samuel Slater's Mill, founded in Providence, Rhode Island, in 1790. Workers at the spinning machines lived in company housing and worked for wages paid in credit at the company store. Cloth itself was not produced at the mill: The yarn was woven into cloth by independent hand weavers working out of their homes.

What kind of employees were recruited to work in the first American cloth factories?
Most of the employees in the early years of the Boston Manufacturing Company were young, unmarried women. Founded at Waltham, Massachusetts, in 1814 by Francis Cabot Lowell, the company ran the first American factories to produce both yarn and finished textiles. Its employees were daughters of New England farmers, usually employed for only a limited period between school and marriage, often to build up their dowries. Housed in supervised boardinghouses, they worked for cash wages at spinning and weaving machines.

How large was the first national debt?

When Secretary of the Treasury Alexander Hamilton restructured the government's miscellaneous debts into more or less their current form in 1791, the national debt was $75 million, or about $18 per person, given the population at that time.

How large is it today?

Nearly 50,000 times larger. The national debt in 1991 was $3.7 trillion, or about $14,500 per person, given the current population.

How many "Banks of the United States" have there been?

Two—both chartered by Congress and both allowed to expire after 20 years. The First Bank of the United States lasted from 1791 to 1811, the second from 1816 to 1836. Each served as the federal government's fiscal agents and repositories of federal funds. The banks were intended to help stabilize fiscal and monetary conditions and were favored by urban commercial interests. The banks were opposed by farmers, entrepreneurs, and state banks, a coalition that helped ensure their demise.

Who were the chief adversaries in the "Bank War"?

On one side of the Bank War (1833–36) was President Andrew Jackson, who wanted to abolish the Second Bank of the United States. On the other side was the Second Bank's president, Nicholas Biddle. Jackson vetoed the Second Bank's early renewal in 1832 and withdrew all federal funds in 1833. In retaliation, Biddle contracted credit and called in loans. After years of public debate, Jackson won the Bank War when its charter was allowed to expire in 1836.

Has the national debt ever been fully paid off?

Only once—in 1835 and 1836, during the presidency of Andrew Jackson. This was the only time any modern nation has eliminated its national debt.

At its height, how much cotton did the South produce?
Between 1850 and 1860, when it was generating 3 to 4.8 million
bales of cotton per year, the South provided over 75 percent of
the cotton in the world.

What was the first installment plan in American business?
It was introduced by Isaac Singer's partner Edward Clark in 1856.
Customers could buy a sewing machine for five dollars down,
paying the rest in monthly installments of three to five dollars,
including interest. Singer was criticized for charging high interest,
but the company's sales took off. In 1857, Clark came up with
another American retail institution: the trade-in allowance, offering 50 dollars for old sewing machines.

In the 19th century, what was the Great Depression?
It was the worldwide period of deflation that lasted from 1873 to
1897 and caused erratic fluctuations in economic activity in the
U.S. Unlike the Great Depression of the 1930s, it was not marked
by low productivity.

**Which administration brought about the first federal income
tax?**
It was during the Lincoln administration in the middle of the Civil
War that the first tax on income was levied by Congress—in the
Internal Revenue Act of 1862. The rates ranged from 3 to 5
percent. Congress eliminated the tax in 1872.

**When did the federal income tax become a permanent insti-
tution?**
It has been permanent since 1913, with the passage of the 16th
Amendment. As established in that year, the bottom rate was 1
percent on taxable net income over $3,000 for an individual,
$4,000 for a married couple. The top rate, for those making more
than $500,000, was 7 percent.

How much did the highest tax bracket fall during the Reagan years?
President Reagan's supply-side tax cuts lowered the top tax rate from 70 percent to 30 percent.

How many shares of stock were traded on Black Tuesday?
On October 29, 1929, the date of the worst crash in Wall Street history, over 16 million shares of stock were traded on the New York Stock Exchange. That day, $8–9 billion in paper value was lost.

How many points did the Dow Jones industrial average fall in the Crash of 1987?
The Dow Jones fell 508 points, or 22.6 percent, on Monday, October 19, 1987.

What was the highest tariff in U.S. history?
It was the Hawley-Smoot Tariff, a 1930 protectionist bill that placed a duty of about 60 percent on imported goods. Aimed at alleviating the Depression, the tariff instead sparked a trade war and worsened economic conditions in the U.S. and Europe.

How much did the national debt grow during World War II?
About sixfold. In 1940, the national debt was $43 billion. At the end of World War II, it was $258.7 billion.

What is the largest denomination of U.S. currency now being issued?
The $100 bill. Issuance of larger denominations stopped in 1969, though some of the bigger bills are still in circulation—all the way up to the $100,000 bill featuring Woodrow Wilson's picture.

What was the leading career choice of Harvard M.B.A. graduates in 1976? In 1986?

In the mid-1970s, the leading career choice for Harvard M.B.A. graduates was manufacturing. Ten years later, it was investment banking.

When did the Dow Jones industrial average first close higher than 1000? 2000? 3000?

Instituted a century ago (in 1896) and named for businessmen Charles Dow and Edward Jones, the economic indicator has set all three records within the last 25 years. It first closed higher than 1000 on Nov. 14, 1972. On January 8, 1987, it closed higher than 2000. Four years later, on April 17, 1991, it finished above 3000.

Did Drexel Burnham Lambert file for bankruptcy in the 1980s or 1990s?

The firm that specialized in using junk bonds to fund 1980s corporate takeovers marked the beginning of a new decade by filing for bankruptcy on February 13, 1990. The company had defaulted on more than $100 million in loans.

How many people serve on the Federal Reserve Board?

Seven members serve on the Board of Governors of the Federal Reserve System, founded in 1913. All are appointed to 14-year terms by the president. The Federal Reserve System, which includes all national banks and many state banks, helps to maintain the country's economic health through such means as fixing reserve deposit requirements and establishing discount rates.

What makes up the GNP (Gross National Product)?

Reported quarterly, it represents the total market value of American goods and services bought for final use during a one-year period. Considered the most comprehensive measure of U.S. economic activity, it includes consumer purchases, private investment, and government spending.

What is the biggest corporation in America?
In 1992, it was General Motors, with sales of $133 billion and assets of $191 billion. In second place was Exxon, with sales of $104 billion and assets of $85 billion.

What magazine empire is bigger, the Hearst Corporation or Time Warner?
As of 1990, Time Warner was about twice as big, with $1.855 billion in magazine revenue to Hearst's $993 million.

What percentage of national wealth is held by the richest one percent of Americans?
More than 36 percent of the nation's net worth (assets minus debts) was held by the top one percent of households in 1989, up from below 20 percent in 1979, according to a 1992 study. The study shows that the wealthiest few increased their share of the nation's total wealth as much during the Reagan years as they did in the 100 years from 1830 to 1929.

What is the official poverty level?
For a family of four, the poverty level defined by the Office of Management and Budget in 1990 is $12,675.

What percentage of Americans live below the poverty level?
In 1990, the percentage of all races was 13.5. Among whites, 10.7 percent lived below the poverty level; among blacks, 31.9 percent did. For persons of Hispanic origin, the rate was 28.1 percent.

Everyday Life

What was the first game played by English colonists?
The first game on record was a game of bowls played in the streets of Jamestown, Virginia, in 1611.

What did "hiving out" mean?
In colonial New England, it meant leaving a town when the rules or the neighbors were not to one's liking and settling somewhere else.

What was a "mechanic" in 18th- and early 19th-century America?
The term referred to a craftsman, such as a potter, blacksmith, or housewright.

What was "redware"?
They were earthenware containers used in 18th- and early 19th-century America for everyday household needs—such as stewpots, mixing bowls, and chamber pots.

What is "sugaring-off"?
Part of the maple-sugar manufacturing process, it refers to boiling down the sap of the maple tree until the sap hardens into candy or crystallizes into sugar. Maple-sugaring was a popular social

activity in America during the 19th century, accompanied by feasting and dancing.

Where did lima beans come from?
The light-green beans were introduced to the U.S. from Lima, Peru, by U.S. Navy Captain John Harris in 1824.

What was the first American restaurant to feature a menu in French and English?
It was the influential continental restaurant Delmonico's, which appeared in New York City in 1837. Although now in a different New York City location, it still operates today.

What are goober peas?
The subject of the Civil War marching song of the same name was peanuts, one of the few foods soldiers in the South could find to eat.

When were standard sizes in clothing first introduced?
Standard sizes for ready-made clothing were not developed until the Civil War, when the Union Army collected body measurements of more than a million conscripts. The statistical data was needed to meet the demand for large numbers of uniforms. From this beginning, fitting systems with numbered sizes were developed during the latter half of the 19th century.

Where did the Elks get their name?
Growing out of a 19th-century social group called the Jolly Cooks, the association now known as the Benevolent and Protective Order of Elks was formed in 1868 from a desire to broaden their pursuits to include patriotism and public service. They chose the name Elk to project a wholly American image and to embody the virtues they saw ascribed to the elk in a natural history book: "fleet of foot, timorous of wrong, but ever ready to combat in defense of self or the female of the species." Currently across the

U.S. there are over 2,200 Elks lodges and 1.4 million brother Elks.

How did Catherine Beecher divide up the housewife's week?
In her popular manual for housewives, *The American Woman's Home,* published with her sister Harriet Beecher Stowe in 1869, Beecher encouraged a systematic and orderly approach to the noble duties of housework. She suggested this schedule:

> Monday—prepare for the week
> Tuesday—wash
> Wednesday—iron
> Thursday—iron, mend, fold and put away clothes
> Friday—sweep and clean the house
> Saturday—arrange things and put them in order
> Sunday—religious duties

What did Americans use before toilet paper was introduced?
Until the late 19th century, Americans used sales catalogues, newspapers, pamphlets, fliers, or whatever other paper they could find. The materials were kept in the bathroom or out-house, where they provided reading matter as well as sanitation. Toilet paper in rolls, sold in plain brown wrappers, was first marketed in the U.S. in the 1880s by Edward and Clarence Scott of Philadelphia.

When was the hot dog introduced to the U.S.?
Originally called a frankfurter (for its origin in Frankfurt, Germany) or a dachshund sausage (for its shape), the food is said to have been first served on a bun in the U.S. in the 1880s. German food vendors Antoine Feuchtwanger in St. Louis, Missouri, and Charles Feltman in Coney Island, Brooklyn, have both been credited with the innovation. The name "hot dog" originated from the cartoons of Hearst sports cartoonist Thomas Aloysius (TAD) Dorgan. About 1900, Dorgan depicted the "red hot" dachshund sau-

sages sold at the New York Polo Grounds as actual dachshunds on buns, with the label "hot dogs."

What is Fletcherism?
It was the theory promoted by late 19th-century businessman Horace Fletcher that extensive chewing, or "mouth thoroughness," would improve one's health. In such books as *Fletcherism: What It Is* and *The ABC of Nutrition,* Fletcher said that every bite of food should be chewed 32 times to "give every tooth of mine a chance." Among Fletcherism's practitioners were Thomas Edison, John D. Rockefeller, and Upton Sinclair.

When was the Boy Scouts of America founded?
It was incorporated in 1910 in Washington, D.C., by painter and illustrator Daniel Carter Beard. Known as "Uncle Dan," Beard based the organization on the British group founded in 1908 by Sir Robert Baden-Powell.

The Girl Scouts?
Juliette Gordon Low founded the organization in Savannah, Georgia, in 1912.

When was the first educational aptitude test developed?
It was developed in 1910 by German-American psychologist Hugo Munsterberg, after he had been asked by William James to direct the psychological laboratory at Harvard University.

When was the SAT first administered?
The College Board first administered the Scholastic Aptitude Test (SAT) in June 1926. More than 8,000 applicants took the test, most of them applicants to elite colleges such as Harvard, Princeton, and Yale. The test, intended to help predict subsequent academic performance, was modeled on intelligence tests administered by the U.S. Army in World War I.

When did the national numbered road system first appear? When did the first freeway appear?

The U.S. government instituted a system of standardized route numbers in 1925 to simplify route directions. Perhaps the nation's most well-known road, Route 66, opened in 1932 to link Chicago and Los Angeles. In December 1940, the first freeway opened—the Arroyo Seco Parkway in Los Angeles. Not until 1956 did the government pass the Federal Aid Highway Act to construct up to 42,500 miles of roads to join metropolitan areas across the country.

Fine Arts and Letters

What was America's first resident opera company?
The New Orleans Opera, which made eight tours to New York and other cities between 1827 and 1845. Specializing in French opera, the company's reputation made New Orleans as synonymous with opera in the 19th century as it was with jazz in the 20th.

How much time did Alexis de Tocqueville spend in America before writing *Democracy in America*?
De Tocqueville based his work on a ten-month visit to study the American prison system for the French government, from May 1831 to February 1832. A study of American social and political institutions, *Democracy in America* was published in two parts in 1835 and 1840.

What was Richard Henry Dana doing before he shipped out as a sailor in the voyage recounted in *Two Years Before the Mast* (1840)?
He was a college student at Harvard. Dana (1815–82) suffered eye problems that led him to go out to sea in hopes of improving his health. Working as a common seaman, he traveled around South America's Cape Horn and collected and cured hides in California. After two years (1834–36), he returned home, went to

law school, and became an advocate for sailors. His autobiographical account of his journey influenced such later writers as Herman Melville and Joseph Conrad.

What is the origin of the name *Pequod* in Herman Melville's *Moby-Dick* (1851)?
The doomed whaling ship commanded by Captain Ahab was named for the Pequot tribe of Connecticut, massacred by English colonists in 1637. Melville said the "celebrated tribe" was "now extinct as the ancient Medes."

Why did American painter James McNeill Whistler sue British art critic John Ruskin?
Whistler (1834–1903) sued Ruskin for libel after Ruskin vilified the painter's *Nocturne in Black and Gold: The Falling Rocket* (1877), accusing Whistler of "flinging a pot of paint in the public's face." Born in Lowell, Massachusetts, Whistler had lived in Europe since 1855 and had become a fixture of London art circles. Whistler won the case but was awarded only a farthing's damages with no costs. The expense of his Pyrrhic victory led him to declare bankruptcy in 1879.

What did Matthew Brady do before becoming a photographer?
Born in upstate New York, Brady (c. 1823–96) worked in New York City as a clerk in the A. T. Stewart department store and as a manufacturer of jewelry cases. He opened his first daguerreotype portrait studio at the corner of Broadway and Fulton Street in 1844. He later became famous for the pictures taken by his corps of Civil War photographers.

What poet was given the title "Laureate of the Confederacy"?
Poet Henry Timrod (1828–67) of Charleston, South Carolina, author of "The Cotton Boll" and "Ethnogenesis."

For what magazine did Winslow Homer illustrate battlefield scenes during the Civil War?
The renowned American painter (1836–1910) worked for *Harper's Weekly* during the Civil War. One of his first important paintings, *Prisoners from the Front* in 1866, drew on this experience.

How long did it take for Emily Dickinson's complete poems to be published in more or less their original form?
An authoritative variorum edition of her poems was not published until Thomas H. Johnson did so in 1955—nearly 70 years after Dickinson's death. Dickinson (1830–86) died with over 1700 poems unpublished; shortly thereafter (in 1890–91), her friends Thomas Wentworth Higginson and Mabel L. Todd began a tradition of publishing her poetry in heavily edited, conventionalized form. Fearful of public reaction, the editors altered her meter and rhyme schemes, metaphors, and syntax, gutting her poetry of much that later generations would appreciate as original.

Which composer premiered a symphony in an American department store?
In 1904, German composer Richard Strauss conducted the world premiere of his work *Symphonia Domestica* in Wanamaker's Department Store in New York City.

What exhibition is credited with introducing modern art to the U.S.?
The Armory Show of 1913, officially known as the International Exhibition of Modern Art. Held in New York City at the 69th Regiment Armory, the gigantic exhibition of about 1,600 works presented much that Americans found new, controversial, and ultimately influential. Contemporary artists represented in the show included Frenchman Marcel Duchamp and Russian Wassily Kandinsky.

When did Isadora Duncan go to Moscow?
The American-born dancer and choreographer (1878–1927), long an advocate of radical politics, went to Moscow in 1921 at the invitation of Anatoly Lunacharsky, Soviet commissar of enlightenment. In Moscow, she founded a school and married poet Sergei Essenin.

How long did Martha Graham choreograph only for women?
The pioneer of modern dance (1894–1991) choreographed for women from 1927 to 1938. She began her own dance troupe in 1929. Her works include *Deep Song* and *Night Journey*.

What era does Frederick Lewis Allen's *Only Yesterday* concern?
A bestseller in its time, the 1931 "informal history" was the first popular recreation of the Jazz Age and the 1920s. The book is still in print.

How close did Gertrude Stein come to being a physician?
The American writer (1874–1946) reached her fourth year at Johns Hopkins Medical School in 1901, but failed several courses and dropped out. After she moved to Paris, her salon served as a gathering place for artists and writers in the 1920s.

> *How close did Walker Percy come to being a physician?*
> The author of such novels as *The Moviegoer* (1961), Percy received an M.D. degree from Columbia but stopped practicing during his internship when he became sick with tuberculosis.

What composition was billed as "An Experiment in Modern Music"?
George Gershwin's *Rhapsody in Blue*, premiered in 1924 by the Paul Whiteman Orchestra. The piece fused symphonic and jazz styles, reflecting Gershwin's background as a popular songwriter.

How much did composer Aaron Copland know about the historical subject of his ballet *Billy the Kid* (1938)?
Very little. Copland admitted that his knowledge of the career of Western outlaw William H. Bonney (1859–81) was "rather vague" and that he "would never have touched it" if he had had to present it realistically. Instead, he treated Billy the Kid as a "young innocent who went wrong, part of the picturesque folklore of the far West."

Did Ernest Hemingway and William Faulkner ever collaborate on a project?
They collaborated indirectly on the 1944 movie version of Hemingway's novel *To Have and Have Not.* Jules Furthman and William Faulkner wrote the screenplay of the film, now best remembered for bringing together Humphrey Bogart and Lauren Bacall. When Hemingway declined to write the screenplay himself, director Howard Hawks reportedly said, "Okay, I'll get Faulkner to do it. He can write better than you can anyway."

When was *Lady Chatterley's Lover* on the bestseller list in the U.S.?
The 1928 novel by British writer D. H. Lawrence was one of the topselling novels of 1959, the year the ban on its publication in the U.S. was lifted.

What was Andy Warhol's real name?
Andy Warhola (1928?–87). Born in Pennsylvania, the painter, graphic artist, and filmmaker was best known for incorporating images from mass culture (such as Marilyn Monroe and Coca-Cola bottles) in the style known as Pop Art.

When was his Campbell's Soup Can *first exhibited?*
The stencilled pictures of Campbell's soup cans brought Warhol his first brush with fame in 1962.

What biography for children did Alice Walker write?
Langston Hughes: American Poet (1974). In it, poet and novelist Walker told the story of her predecessor in the African-American literary tradition. Hughes was at the center of the influential Harlem Renaissance of the 1920s. Walker is known for such works as the novel *The Color Purple* (1982).

What American writer said, "I don't think any novelist should be concerned with literature"?
Jacqueline Susann (1918–74), the immensely successful author of such fiction bestsellers as *Valley of the Dolls* (1966), *The Love Machine* (1969), and *Once Is Not Enough* (1973).

What Cincinatti official was indicted on obscenity charges for exhibiting photographs by the late Robert Mapplethorpe?
Dennis Barrie, director of the Contemporary Arts Center in Cincinnati, Ohio, was indicted by a local grand jury but acquitted on October 5, 1990.

Firsts

What was the first theatrical performance in America north of Mexico?
It took place in 1598 in a Spanish settlement near present-day El Paso, Texas. The play was a comedy about a military expedition.

What was the first college to be founded in America north of Mexico?
It was a college for young men founded by French Jesuits at Quebec in 1635. Harvard, the first college in the British colonies, was founded in 1636.

What was the first written constitution in the U.S.?
It was the *Fundamental Orders*, written for the Connecticut Colony at its founding in 1639. This document is considered the first written constitution not only in the U.S. but the world.

What was the first magazine created in America?
Two Philadelphia-based political periodicals, both published in February 1741, share the honor. One was the *American Magazine*, or *A Monthly View of the Political State of the British Colonies*, published by Andrew Bradford. The other was the *General Magazine, and Historical Chronicle, For all the British Plantations*, published by Benjamin Franklin. Both folded within a year.

What were the first three states admitted to the union after the original 13?
They were:

Vermont—1791, created from parts of New York and New Hampshire
Kentucky—1792, created from Virginia
Tennessee—1796, created from North Carolina

What was the first American cookbook?
It was the 1796 collection *American Cookery* by Amelia Simmons, whose pen name was "An American Orphan." Four editions of the book appeared between 1796 and 1808.

When and where was the first U.S. federal prison established?
The first one opened in Auburn, New York in 1821. To regulate prisoner activity, Auburn employed what came to be known as the Auburn system. In the hopes of instilling discipline and effecting rehabilitation, the Auburn system required inmates to work silently in groups. When not working, inmates were confined in silence to individual cells to meditate on their crimes. Economical and labor efficient, the Auburn system became a popular method of imprisonment in the U.S.

What was the first U.S. warship to make a trip around the world?
It was the sloop-of-war *Vincennes* in 1829–31, during the administration of President Andrew Jackson. Jackson used the show of force to protect American commerce in the Pacific.

What was the first attempted assassination of a president?
It took place in January 1835, when a house painter named Richard Lawrence aimed two pistols at Andrew Jackson. Both guns misfired.

What was the first assassination of a president?
John Wilkes Booth's assassination of Abraham Lincoln in 1865.

What was the first American steam railroad to carry both passengers and freight?

It was the Baltimore & Ohio Railroad, which began operation in 1830, powered by the Tom Thumb locomotive built by American manufacturer Peter Cooper (1791–1883).

Who was the first president photographed while in office?

James K. Polk, photographed by Matthew Brady in 1849.

Who is the first president of whom there is any known photograph?
John Quincy Adams.

Which Wright brother was the first person to fly in an airplane?

Orville made the first flight in the airplane built by him and his brother Wilbur, on December 17, 1903, at Kitty Hawk, North Carolina. The 12-horsepower biplane covered 120 feet in 12 seconds.

Who was the first Socialist elected to the U.S. Senate?

Wisconsin's Victor Berger, elected in 1911.

What was the first movie shown in the White House?

D. W. Griffith's *Birth of a Nation* in 1916. Woodrow Wilson was president at the time.

Who was the first person to receive a Social Security check?

Vermont widow Ida May Fuller received the first Social Security check in 1940. The check totalled $22.54.

When was the first atomic-powered submarine launched?
The *Nautilus* was launched at Groton, Connecticut, on June 21, 1954.

When did the first domestic jet airliner passenger service in the U.S. open?
National Airlines began it on December 10, 1958, between New York and Miami.

What was the first Zen Buddhist monastery in the U.S.?
Tassajara, founded in Big Sur, California, in 1967 by Richard Baker and Zen master Shunryu Suzuki.

Who participated in the first vice-presidential debate?
Democratic candidate Walter Mondale and Republican candidate Robert Dole took part in the debate during the 1976 Carter-Ford presidential contest.

Who flew the first mission in the U.S. space shuttle program?
Captain Robert L. Crippen and John W. Young flew the space shuttle *Columbia* on its maiden voyage April 12–14, 1981.

Foreign Affairs

Did the U.S. and France ever go to war with each other?
Yes and no. From 1798 to 1800, the U.S. and France clashed in
a series of naval hostilities but never formally declared war. At
issue was France's resentment at what it viewed as American
partiality to France's enemy Britain. The U.S. was angry because
French privateers had been seizing American ships and the French
foreign minister had demanded a bribe in return for peace talks.
After two years of clashes at sea, an agreement with new French
leader Napoleon Bonaparte ended the "quasi-war."

What did the Rush-Bagot convention settle?
This 1817 exchange of notes between U.S. Secretary of State
Richard Rush and British Minister Charles Bagot provided for
disarmament of the U.S-Canada frontier. It laid the basis for
keeping the boundary undefended to this day.

What was the Monroe Doctrine?
Formulated in 1823 by President James Monroe and Secretary of
State John Quincy Adams, it warned that the U.S. would not
tolerate new colonization of the Americas by European powers,
while promising that the U.S. would not interfere with existing
colonies or with European governments.

What was the Roosevelt Corollary?
President Theodore Roosevelt's 1904 corollary to the Monroe Doctrine said that the U.S. could itself intervene in Latin America to correct what it considered "chronic wrongdoing."

When did Commodore Perry first visit Japan?
Commodore Matthew Calbraith Perry first brought an armed squadron to Tokyo Bay in 1853, when he delivered a letter from President Millard Fillmore to the emperor of Japan. In 1854, on a second expedition, Perry succeeded in persuading the Japanese to open their previously isolated society to U.S. trade.

Have any treaties ending foreign wars ever been signed in the U.S.?
Only one. In 1905, Portsmouth, New Hampshire, was the site of the treaty that ended the Russo-Japanese War. President Theodore Roosevelt facilitated the negotiations between Japan and Russia.

Who was first associated with the term "dollar diplomacy"?
The practice of using economic means to achieve foreign policy goals was first associated with President William Howard Taft (served 1909–13) and his Secretary of State Philander C. Knox.

How long did the U.S. occupy Haiti?
The U.S. took military control of the bankrupt republic in 1915. Two decades later, in 1934, after instituting public works and financial reform, both civilian and military forces were removed.

In what treaty did the U.S. agree to outlaw war?
In the Kellogg-Briand Pact, signed on August 27, 1928, the U.S., France, Great Britain, Japan, Italy, Belgium, Czechoslovakia, and Poland all agreed to give up war as an instrument of foreign policy. However, the treaty lacked enforcement power, and within 14 years all the parties that signed it were fighting in World War II.

Who was the pact named for?
President Calvin Coolidge's Secretary of State Frank Kellogg
and French foreign minister Aristide Briand.

What were President Franklin Roosevelt's "Four Freedoms"?
In his January 6, 1941, message to Congress, Roosevelt called for
a world where these "Four Freedoms" were protected: freedom of
speech and expression, freedom of religion, freedom from want,
and freedom from fear.

How many nations first joined the United Nations?
Fifty-one nations, including the U.S., signed the U.N. charter in
1945. The charter was framed at a conference in San Francisco.

How old is the CIA?
Founded in 1947, the CIA was born about the same time as the
Cold War between the U.S. and the Soviet Union. An offshoot of
World War II's Office of Strategic Services (OSS), the agency was
established to gather foreign intelligence, carry out counterintel-
ligence, and perform covert operations.

Who signed his name as "X" to the article in the magazine *Foreign Affairs* that first outlined the policy of containing Soviet expansion?
George K. Kennan, then a member of the State Department's
policy planning staff, wrote the pseudonymous article in 1947.

How much did the Marshall Plan cost?
The four-year post-World War II economic recovery plan for
Europe cost $13 billion. The plan, enacted 1948–51, was named
for its chief architect, U.S. Secretary of State George C. Marshall.

What country received the most aid under the Marshall Plan?
Great Britain, with $3.1 billion, received the most; Iceland, with

$32 million, received the least. The aid came in the form of grants, food, goods, and tariff reductions.

How long did the Berlin Airlift last?
For ten months in 1948 and 1949, 1,000 planes of the Western powers flew food, fuel, and other necessities to the two million civilians in West Berlin, then under a Soviet blockade.

Was John Foster Dulles for or against the containment policy?
Dulles, secretary of state under Dwight D. Eisenhower from 1953 to 1959, often expressed his belief that the containment policy of the Truman years did not go far enough. In the 1952 presidential campaign, he called for a "rollback" of Soviet domination of Eastern Europe and the "unleashing" of Taiwanese leader Chiang Kai-shek. Despite his tough talk, Dulles upheld the principles of containment during his term in office.

What U.S. presidential administration initiated the plan for the Bay of Pigs invasion?
It was not John F. Kennedy's but Dwight D. Eisenhower's administration that first launched plans for the overthrow of Fidel Castro, the Communist leader of Cuba, by an armed invasion of Cuban exiles. Kennedy, who came to office in January 1961, allowed the plan to go forward. On April 17, a force of about 2,000 Cuban exiles attacked at Bahía de Cochinos (Bay of Pigs) in Cuba. Within three days they were forced to surrender.

Who was the first director of the Peace Corps?
Sargent Shriver, husband of President Kennedy's sister Eunice and, in 1972, the running mate of unsuccessful presidential candidate George McGovern. The Peace Corps, a volunteer organization to help Third World countries, was founded by Kennedy's executive order on March 1, 1961.

When was the "hot line" first set up between the chief executives of the U.S. and the U.S.S.R.?

The emergency communications link between Washington and Moscow was installed in 1963 to reduce the possibility of accidental nuclear war.

When were the following nuclear arms treaties signed:
   Limited Test Ban Treaty—August 1963
   Antiballistic Missile Treaty—May 1972
   Strategic Arms Limitation Treaty (SALT)—June 1979
   Strategic Arms Reduction Treaty (START) I—July 1991
   Strategic Arms Reduction Treaty (START) II—January 1993

For whom is the "Boland Amendment" named?
The 1982 law prohibiting federal support for the contra rebels in Nicaragua was introduced by Massachusetts representative Edward Boland. In 1987, Marine Colonel Oliver North and national security chief John Poindexter were accused of violating the Boland Amendment by diverting funds to the contras from the sale of arms to Iran.

Getting Bigger

What were the boundaries of the U.S. at independence?
According to the 1783 Treaty of Paris, in which Great Britain acknowledged American independence, the new nation's boundaries were the Great Lakes, the Mississippi River, the state of Florida and the latitude line of 31° North.

What was the "Old Northwest"?
In the early United States, it represented much of what we would now call the Midwest. Organized as the Northwest Territory in 1787, it was the area bounded by the Appalachian Mountains, the Great Lakes, and the Mississippi and Ohio Rivers. Britain had acquired it from France in the French and Indian War, then passed it on to the United States. In time it became the states of Ohio, Indiana, Illinois, Michigan, and Wisconsin, and part of Minnesota.

What was the cost of the Louisiana Purchase?
The 1803 purchase from France of 828,000 square miles of land, stretching from the Mississippi River to the Rocky Mountains, cost $15 million. This put the price of each acre of land at about 3 cents.

How much did Alaska cost?
The purchase of Alaska from Russia in 1867 cost $7.2 million. This made the selling price of each acre about 2 cents.

How much did the U.S. government give Lewis and Clark for their expedition?

In 1803, the U.S. Congress granted $2,500 for an expedition to explore the territory west of the Mississippi River. Selected by President Thomas Jefferson to lead the group of 50 people were Meriwether Lewis and William Clark. Starting out from St. Louis, Missouri, the expedition crossed the Rockies and reached the Pacific coast of what is now Oregon before returning to St. Louis in 1806.

When did the U.S. acquire Florida?

In 1819, Spain ceded Florida to the U.S. for $5 million. In addition, Spain gave up its claim to the Oregon Territory while the U.S. recognized that Texas belonged to Spain. Within three decades, in 1845, the U.S. had annexed Texas too.

When did Texas try to capture New Mexico?

In 1841, an expedition of 300 people from the Republic of Texas (independent from 1836 to 1845) traveled to Santa Fe to encourage New Mexicans to revolt against Mexico. The Texans failed to convince anyone to revolt and were imprisoned as invaders. They were only released after strong protests from the U.S. and Britain.

What was the "Mexican cession"?

This was the territory Mexico called the "Far North," including what are today California, Nevada, Utah, most of New Mexico and Arizona, and parts of Wyoming and Colorado. In return Mexico received $15 million, was set free of $3 million in American claims, and got rid of American forces occupying its capital. The land cession was part of the Treaty of Guadalupe Hidalgo on February 2, 1848, ending the Mexican War.

What was the cost of the Gadsden Purchase?

The southern parts of present-day Arizona and New Mexico were purchased from Mexico for $10 million in 1853. The deal was negotiated for the U.S. by railroad president James Gadsden.

Where did the Oregon Trail run?
The road used by migrants moving westward in the mid-19th century ran about 2,000 miles from Independence or Westport, Missouri, to Oregon's Willamette Valley. It took about six months for wagon trains to cover the distance. The Oregon Trail was in use from the 1840s until the advent of the railroads in the 1870s.

When was the U.S. frontier officially closed?
In 1890. That was the year in which the Bureau of the Census announced there was no difference between frontier and settlement—meaning that the frontier was now closed.

How did Puerto Rico become an American possession?
The United States took over the island from Spain in 1898 as a result of the Spanish-American War. Since 1917, Puerto Ricans have been considered U.S. citizens. Since 1952, the island has been a self-governing commonwealth, voluntarily associated with the U.S.

Do residents of Guam vote in American national elections?
The people of Guam are U.S. citizens but do not vote in national elections. The U.S. acquired Guam from Spain in 1898. Since 1950, the island (the largest of the Marianas Islands, located east of the Philippines) has been self-governing.

What is American Samoa's status vis-à-vis the U.S.?
Acquired in 1900, the group of islands south of Hawaii is an unincorporated territory of the U.S. administered by the Department of the Interior.

Which became a state first, Alaska or Hawaii?
Alaska became the 49th state in 1958, Hawaii the 50th in 1959.

Government and
Politics

Who was the first postmaster general of the United States?
The Continental Congress appointed Benjamin Franklin to that
position in 1775. In 1789, Samuel Osgood was named the first
postmaster general under the new Constitution.

What was the Great Compromise?
This was the agreement reached at the Philadelphia Constitutional Convention in 1787 to give each state two senators and to
apportion seats in the House of Representatives on the basis of
population. The agreement satisfied both the smaller, less popu-
lous states, which wanted all states to be represented equally, and
the larger states, which wanted representation to reflect population.

**What duties does the Constitution assign to the vice-
president?**
To be president of the Senate; to cast a tie-breaking vote in the
Senate when needed; and to replace the president of the U.S. in
the event that the latter's term ends prematurely.

How many *Federalist Papers* appeared in newspapers?
Eighty-five essays were published in New York City newspapers
from October 27, 1787, to August 16, 1788. Written by Alexan-

der Hamilton, James Madison, and John Jay, *The Federalist Papers* (or *The Federalist*) supported the proposed Constitution and up-held the need for a strong central government.

What were the last states to ratify the Constitution?
The required nine of the thirteen states ratified the Constitution between January and June 1788. But it was not until after Wash-ington was inaugurated in 1789 that all of the states ratified it. The last stragglers were North Carolina in November 1789 and Rhode Island in May 1790.

When was New York City the capital of the U.S.?
It was named the capital of the country in 1788 and remained so until 1800, when Washington, D.C. was so named.

What was the first political party in America?
It was the Federalist Party, founded in 1790 by Alexander Ham-ilton and John Adams. Around the same time, Thomas Jefferson built a rival organization that became known as the Republican or Democratic-Republican Party.

Who was the "Gerry" behind gerrymandering?
Elbridge Gerry, a signer of the Declaration of Independence. In 1812, when Gerry was the Republican governor of Massachusetts, legislators from his party redrew district lines to favor their rep-resentatives. Their rivals, the Federalists, blamed Gerry for the redistricting (though he was actually opposed to it). A Federalist cartoonist portrayed a warped district as a salamander, and called it a "Gerrymander." The name became a common term for draw-ing districts to suit political advantage.

What war did the "War Hawks" call for?
The young Republican congressmen from southern and western states, including Henry Clay of Kentucky and John C. Calhoun of South Carolina, demanded war against Great Britain in 1810–11.

They got their wish in the War of 1812. Dubbed "War Hawks" by their opponents, they wanted to stop Great Britain from impressing American sailors and blockading American ports. They also had hopes of expanding into Canada (owned by Britain) and Florida and Texas (owned by Britain's ally Spain).

Who were the candidates the last time the presidential election went to the House of Representatives?
In 1824, they were Andrew Jackson, John Quincy Adams, William H. Crawford, and Henry Clay. Jackson won a plurality of both the electoral and popular votes, but not a majority in the Electoral College. In accord with the Constitution, the election was decided by the House of Representatives, which chose Adams. Jackson got his revenge when he defeated Adams for reelection four years later.

Who was the first presidential candidate of the Democratic Party?
Andrew Jackson in 1828. He won.

Who was the first presidential candidate of the modern Republican Party?
John C. Frémont in 1856. He lost to Democrat James Buchanan. The first victorious Republican presidential candidate was Abraham Lincoln in 1860.

Why did the Whig Party in the U.S. call themselves Whigs?
Formed in 1834 to oppose President Andrew Jackson, the party took its name from the British antimonarchical party, the Whigs, to underline their conflict with the man they viewed as "King Andrew." The word "Whig" itself was an old pejorative term meaning "cattle-driver." In the 1836 presidential election, the party offered three regional candidates—Daniel Webster, for the northeast, Hugh Lawson White for the south, and William Henry

Harrison for the west. They were all defeated by Jackson's successor, Martin Van Buren.

When did U.S. political parties first develop party platforms at their nominating conventions?
The first platform was negotiated by the Democratic Party for the 1840 election.

Who was Wilmot and what was his proviso?
David Wilmot was a congressman from Pennsylvania who in 1846 proposed an amendment to a military appropriations bill that slavery be forbidden in any territory obtained from Mexico during or after the Mexican War (1846–48). The amendment passed in the House but not the Senate.

Where did the "Know Nothings" get their name?
The secretive, anti-Catholic, and antiforeign movement, which flourished in the 1850s, received its name because members, when questioned by outsiders, answered, "I know nothing." They pursued their aims through electoral politics, violence, and intimidation. Also known as the Order of the Star-Spangled Banner and the American Party, the movement had adherents in Boston, New York, Baltimore, St. Louis, and elsewhere.

How many debates were held by Lincoln and Douglas?
The two candidates for the U.S. Senate in Illinois in 1858, Abraham Lincoln and Stephen Douglas, held seven debates.

Who won that election?
Democrat Douglas was reelected. But Lincoln's strong performance in the campaign led to his nomination as the Republican candidate for president in 1860.

What did the Mugwumps stand for?
The independent political party was comprised of Republicans

who wanted to band together to demonstrate support for the Democratic candidate for the 1884 election, Grover Cleveland. They remained active in presidential politics through 1892. The word mugwump was a slang term for "kingpin."

Who was the last president to be elected without winning the largest share of the popular vote?
Benjamin Harrison, Republican, in 1888. Fewer ballots were cast for him at the polling booth than for Democrat Grover Cleveland. But Harrison carried the day by winning 233 votes in the Electoral College to Cleveland's 168.

Was the man behind the "Sherman Anti-Trust Act" related to the man behind "Sherman's March to the Sea"?
Yes. The Sherman Anti-Trust Act, passed in 1890, was sponsored by John Sherman, the younger brother of William Tecumseh Sherman. It was the latter Sherman who, as a Union general, led the destructive march across Georgia in 1864, ravaging the countryside from Atlanta to Savannah.

What was the first known case of wiretapping in American politics?
It occurred at the Republican convention in Chicago in 1912, when opponents of Teddy Roosevelt tapped the phones he used to communicate with his managers. When Roosevelt learned of it, he left his home in Oyster Bay, New York, and came to Chicago to talk to his managers without benefit of phone.

When did the U.S. government first adopt daylight saving time?
In 1918, during World War I. During daylight saving time, which currently extends from the first Sunday in April to the last Sunday in October, clocks are set ahead one hour to extend daylight hours into the late afternoon and evening.

What was Teapot Dome?
Located in Wyoming, it was one of two naval oil reserve sites improperly leased in 1922 to private oil companies by Albert B. Fall, President Harding's secretary of the interior. After the scandal broke in 1923, Fall paid a heavy fine and served a year in prison for bribery. The other oil reserve site implicated in the scandal was Elk Hills, California.

Who were the brains in Franklin Delano Roosevelt's brain trust?
The intellectuals who served as advisers to FDR included attorney Basil O'Connor, Felix Frankfurter of Harvard Law School, and Raymond Moley, Rexford Tugwell, and Adolf Berle of Columbia University. The nickname for the elite group who helped shape the New Deal was first suggested in 1932 by Roosevelt's legal counsel Samuel Rosenman.

How many men worked in the Civilian Conservation Corps?
In its nine years of existence (1933–42), the employment program for men between 18 and 24 put over 2 million men to work conserving and developing the country's natural resources.

What state did Joseph McCarthy represent?
Wisconsin. The Republican senator, famous for his investigations of alleged communists, served in the Senate from 1946 to 1957.

Who were Adlai Stevenson's running mates in the 1952 and 1956 elections?
John Sparkman in 1952 and Estes Kefauver in 1956. Stevenson lost both times to Dwight Eisenhower and his running mate Richard Nixon.

How many times have the major political parties held their national conventions in Los Angeles?

Only once. The Democratic Party nominated John F. Kennedy in Los Angeles in July 1960.

When were the residents of Washington, D.C., allowed to vote in presidential elections?
Not until the 23rd Amendment was ratified in 1961.

How long has the Electoral College remained at its present number of members?
There have been 538 members of the Electoral College since 1964, when, in keeping with the 23rd Amendment, the District of Columbia acquired three electors. In addition, each state chooses as many electors as it has senators and representatives in Congress.

> *How many electoral votes are needed to win?*
> At present, 270—a majority of the 538 electors.

What Republican presidential candidate employed the slogan, "In your heart you know he's right"?
Barry Goldwater in 1964. Some Democratic opponents responded, "In your guts you know he's nuts." Public fear that Goldwater was an extremist helped Lyndon Johnson defeat him that year.

When was Medicare established?
Federally funded health insurance for the disabled and those over 65 was part of the Social Security Amendments of 1965. The Amendments also saw the beginning of Medicaid.

Why was Amtrak founded?
The federal government founded the National Rail Passenger Corporation in 1970 to prevent the imminent extinction of passenger railroads in the U.S. Unable to compete with airlines, the com-

mercial railroads had been eliminating most of their passenger service and concentrating on freight. Railroad passenger-miles traveled in a single year had declined from a height of 95.7 billion in 1944 to 10.8 billion in 1970. Operating with government subsidies, Amtrak has since continued to transport passengers along a limited number of the old commercial routes.

What is the most recent amendment to the Constitution?
It is the 26th Amendment, which lowered the voting age to 18. The amendment was ratified on July 1, 1971, in response to the demand of young Americans that those old enough to be drafted be old enough to vote.

What presidential candidate carried the most states in a general election?
Richard Nixon in 1972 and Ronald Reagan in 1984 are tied for the honor, with 49 states each.

In what post did Caspar Weinberger serve under President Nixon?
Weinberger, who went on to become Ronald Reagan's secretary of defense (1981–87), served as secretary of health, education, and welfare (1973–75) under both Nixon and Ford.

How well did George Wallace do in the 1968 presidential election?
The "American Independent" candidate, with his running mate Curtis LeMay, got 13.6 percent of the popular vote and 8.6 percent of the electoral vote. Richard Nixon won against both Wallace and Hubert Humphrey.

How many electoral votes did independent candidate John Anderson get in 1980?
None—but he did win 6.6 percent of the popular vote.

What about Ross Perot in 1992?
Perot won no electoral votes but got 19 percent of the popular vote.

How old was Bill Clinton when he was first elected governor of Arkansas?

The future U.S. president was elected governor in 1978 at the age of 32, making him the youngest person to hold that office in Arkansas history. Two years later, he was voted out; he regained the governorship in 1982. Clinton became president in 1993.

Inventions

What does a cotton gin do?
The 1793 invention by Eli Whitney mechanically removed seeds from a cotton bloom without harming its fiber. Previously, seeds had to be removed laboriously by hand. The invention led to an economic boom for the South by increasing the amount of cotton the southern states could provide to textile manufacturers. It also cemented Southern dependence on the slaves who picked the raw cotton.

Was there a John Deere?
Yes. In 1839, he invented the steel plow, which, along with Cyrus McCormick's 1834 invention, the reaper, changed the face of American agriculture.

Where did the first telegraph line run?
Invented by Samuel F. B. Morse and completed in 1844, the telegraph line ran from Washington, D.C., to Baltimore, Maryland. The first message, telegraphed on May 24, 1844, was, "What hath God wrought!"

Where was the first oil well?
The first petroleum well was dug by American railway conductor Edwin L. Drake on August 28, 1859, at Titusville in western

Pennsylvania. Kerosene for lamps was the first product to be refined from oil; gasoline did not become important until the development of the internal combustion engine in the 1880s and '90s.

What made the Colt revolver different from previous handguns?

Previous handguns could fire only once before they had to be reloaded. Samuel Colt's invention, patented in 1835, had a six-chambered cylinder that rotated with each shot, automatically readying another bullet for firing. The Colt revolver became standard equipment on America's western frontier.

In what war was the Gatling gun first used?

Precursor of the modern machine gun, the rapid-firing weapon saw limited action during the Civil War, specifically in the Petersburg Campaign in 1864. The hand-crank-operated gun, capable of firing hundreds of rounds a minute, was patented by Richard J. Gatling in 1862.

When was the telephone first shown to the public?

Alexander Graham Bell first displayed his electric telephone in 1876 at the Centennial Exhibition in Philadelphia, Pennsylvania.

What did Thomas Edison use as a filament in the first successful electric light bulb?

After experimenting with thousands of materials, Edison discovered in 1879 that a scorched cotton thread, the equivalent of a carbon wire, was the filament he needed—one that would glow for a long period without melting. Edison's discovery ushered in the age of electric lighting.

Who filed suit against the Wright brothers over the design of their airplanes?

In 1914, Glenn Curtis fought the Wright brothers for patent rights on the airplane. The U.S. court decided in favor of the Wright brothers.

What was the first commercially successful plastic?

It was celluloid, developed by American John Wesley Hyatt in 1869 from a material that had first been produced by British chemist Alexander Parkes in 1855. Hyatt originally intended the synthetic organic substance as a cheap alternative to ivory for the manufacture of billiard balls, but other commercial uses were soon found for it—most notably as film stock for photographic negatives and motion pictures. However, celluloid's poor performance under extremes of heat and cold doomed it as a material for common household items.

Who invented the Richter magnitude scale?

Charles F. Richter of the California Institute of Technology developed the scale in 1935 as a mathematical device to compare the sizes of earthquakes. Each whole number increase in the scale corresponds to a tenfold increase in the amplitude of waves measured by a seismograph—or an increase of about 31 times the energy of a quake that is one number smaller.

Who invented nylon?

Du Pont chemist Wallace Hume Carrothers invented the artificial polymer in the 1930s while searching for alternatives to silk. Nylon stockings first came on the market with heavy publicity on what was billed as "Nylon Day," May 15, 1940. Women hungry for a cheap and durable alternative to silk stockings bought millions of pairs by the end of the year.

Where was the first nuclear reactor?

In a squash court at the University of Chicago. There, using a uranium-235-based reactor, Italian-American physicist Enrico Fermi achieved the first sustained nuclear chain reaction on December 2, 1942, a crucial step in the development of nuclear weapons and nuclear power.

When was the Salk polio vaccine first used on school children?

The inoculation campaign during the polio epidemic first started in Pittsburgh, Pennsylvania, in 1954. Dr. Jonas Salk, the developer of the vaccine, himself was involved in the first program of mass inoculation. The oral polio vaccine, developed in 1956 by Albert Sabin, became more widely used than inoculations.

What was the name of the first commercially available oral contraceptive?

The first "pill" was introduced in August 1960, by Chicago-based pharmaceutical company G. D. Searle. It contained synthetic progesterone and estrogen and was named Enovid 10.

Labor History

What was the average amount of time served by an indentured servant?
The average time the 17th- and 18th-century peasants and laborers spent to pay off the debt incurred by their passage to America (about $100) was four years.

What was the first labor union in America?
It was the Federal Society of Journeymen Cordwainers (shoemakers), formed in Philadelphia, Pennsylvania, in 1794.

What was Samuel Gompers's (1850–1924) occupation before he became a labor leader?
The founder of the American Federation of Labor (AFL) was, like his father, a cigar maker. The English immigrant reshaped the Cigar Makers International Union before founding the AFL in 1886.

When was the first eight-hour day introduced in America?
It was instituted for federal employees in public work projects in 1868. Before the law was passed, an average workday could run 10 to 12 hours. In 1867, the Illinois state legislature had passed a law proclaiming the eight-hour day to be "the legal workday in the state." But the law lacked enforcement procedures and em-

ployers refused to follow it. Strikes against company owners were eventually suppressed and workers soon resumed a 10-hour day.

For what practical reasons did Henry Ford adopt the eight-hour day and five-day week?

He did it to alleviate a depression in the auto industry in 1926. The move to reduce working hours curbed overproduction and unemployment in the industry.

Who were the Molly Maguires?

They were a secret militant organization of Irish miners working in the Pennsylvania anthracite coal mines in the 19th century. They organized in 1854 to fight the mine operators. In 1875, a Pinkerton spy working for the owners infiltrated the group. That led to the conviction and hanging of 20 Molly Maguires on charges of blackmail and death threats against mine officials. With a number of other Molly Maguires imprisoned, the organization fell apart.

What business was the target of the Homestead strike?

The five-month strike was begun in July 1892 by workers at Andrew Carnegie's steelworks in Homestead, Pennsylvania. It began when Carnegie refused to recognize the workers' right to negotiate as a union. Steelworks manager Henry Clay Frick brought in 300 Pinkerton guards to break the strike, but the workers drove them off in a bloody day of fighting on July 6. The strike was finally broken by 8,000 state militiamen sent in by the governor.

When did Labor Day become a national holiday?

In 1894, a U.S. congressional resolution made it a legal holiday. Promoted by the Knights of Labor since 1887, the holiday had already been celebrated in several states.

What was the official name of the Wobblies?
The Industrial Workers of the World, or IWW. Founded in Chicago in 1905 and composed mostly of unskilled workers, the union advocated direct action to further the cause of worker control of the means of production. Their aim was to create "one big union" for all workers.

What was IWW leader Joe Hill's last request before his execution?
Imprisoned for nearly two years after a questionable 1914 murder conviction in Utah, Hill was executed on November 14, 1915. The night before the execution, he cabled friend and IWW cofounder "Big Bill" Haywood, "Don't waste any time in mourning. Organize."

Where was the first major sit-down strike?
The practice of ceasing to work but occupying the workplace first occurred on a mass scale in the rubber factories of Akron, Ohio, in 1936. Sit-down strikes in Flint, Michigan, and Cleveland, Ohio, followed. In 1939, the Supreme Court ruled sit-down strikes illegal.

What was the first African-American union?
The Brotherhood of Sleeping Car Porters, founded in 1925 by A. Philip Randolph and other labor leaders. The Pullman Company, at first opposed to the Brotherhood, awarded the union its first contract in 1937. Later the Brotherhood became best known for its civil rights activism.

When were cost-of-living raises first worked into union contracts?
The raises, based on the U.S. cost-of-living index, were first negotiated into General Motors-United Auto Workers Union contracts in 1948.

What was the combined membership of the AFL and the CIO when the two unions merged?
The two largest U.S. labor unions, the American Federation of Labor and the Congress of Industrial Organizations, became the AFL-CIO on December 5, 1955. The merger created a combined membership estimated at 15 million.

When and where was the first U.S. strike by doctors?
In 1975, physicians at New York City hospitals engaged in a work slowdown to request shorter hours.

How many air traffic controllers did President Reagan fire during the strike in 1981?
He fired all of the 11,600 strikers after they refused to obey a court order to return to work. By decade's end, there were 2,500 fewer air traffic controllers employed in the industry. Meanwhile, U.S. air traffic had increased by a third and safety records had worsened.

Landmarks and Symbols

What is the inscription on the Tomb of the Unknown Soldier in Arlington National Cemetery?
It reads: "Here Rests in Honored Glory an American Soldier Known But to God." Arlington has been a military cemetery since 1864.

How many stars, arrows, olive leaves, and olives are there in the Great Seal of the United States?
There are 13 of each—symbolizing the original 13 colonies. The design of the seal was approved by Congress in 1782. As seen on the back of the dollar bill, the seal consists of an eagle holding olives and arrows in its talons, with stars in a nimbus over its head. In its beak, the eagle holds a banner with the Latin inscription *E pluribus unum* ("Out of many, one"). The number of letters in that motto is also 13.

Who founded the Library of Congress?
The principal founder was Thomas Jefferson, who believed that a democratic legislative body needed a source of information and scholarship on every subject. It was established by Congress on April 24, 1800. Originally based in the Capitol in Washington, D.C., it was moved into a separate building in 1897.

How many items are in the collections of the Library of Congress?
More than 97 million—including books, films, photographs, manuscripts, and records.

What was the name of the poem that later became the "Star-Spangled Banner"?
The poem written by Francis Scott Key in 1814 to commemorate the battle for Fort McHenry, Maryland, during the War of 1812, was called "Defence of Fort M'Henry."

How many stanzas does "The Star-Spangled Banner" have?
The song has four stanzas, all ending with "O'er the land of the free, and the home of the brave." Congress made it the national anthem in 1931.

Which took longer to build, the Erie Canal or the Panama Canal?
The Panama Canal, which required ten years from start to finish, took two years longer than the Erie Canal. Excavation on the 51-mile long Panama Canal began in 1904; the first ship entered the waterway in 1914. The Erie Canal, linking Buffalo and Albany, New York, took from 1817 to 1825 to complete.

Who wrote "My Country 'Tis of Thee"?
Rev. Samuel F. Smith wrote the lyrics for this song (also called "America") to the music of the British national anthem, "God Save the King" in Amherst, Massachusetts, in 1832.

What vessel was nicknamed "Old Ironsides"?
The *Constitution,* a 44-gun frigate that defeated two British warships in the War of 1812. It was memorialized as "Old Ironsides" in the 1830 poem of that name by Oliver Wendell Holmes, written to protest the proposed scrapping of the ship. The ship was

saved and, in rebuilt form, is still on view at the Boston Navy Yard.

Was the Smithsonian Institution named for an American?
No. Founded in 1846, it was named for British chemist James Smithson (1765–1829), who bequeathed his fortune to build the U.S. institution. It is now the world's largest museum complex, containing 14 museums and the National Zoo.

What is the official name of the Statue of Liberty?
"Liberty Enlightening the World." A gift from France, the statue was designed by Frédéric Auguste Bartholdi and dedicated in New York harbor in 1886.

When was the Emma Lazarus poem "The New Colossus" added to the Statue of Liberty?
Emma Lazarus (1849–87), a New York Jewish poet, wrote the poem with its words, "Give me your tired, your poor/ Your huddled masses yearning to breathe free," in honor of the planned statue in 1883, but the poem was not part of the statue when it was unveiled in 1886. In 1903, an admirer of Lazarus named Georgina Schuyler arranged to have the poem placed on a bronze plaque inside the statue. Not until 1945 was the plaque moved from the interior of the statue to its main entrance.

When did Ellis Island open?
The island in Upper New York Bay, named for its former owner Sam Ellis, operated as an immigration center from 1892 to 1943. It was a detention place for deportees until 1954. In 1965 it became part of the Statue of Liberty National Monument. Following restoration of its Registry Room, the point of entry for immigrants, Ellis Island was rededicated in 1990 as a people's museum.

What was the original text of the Pledge of Allegiance?

As written by Francis Bellamy, editor of *The Youth's Companion*, where is first appeared on September 8, 1892, the pledge read: "I pledge allegiance to my Flag and the Republic for which it stands; one nation indivisible, with liberty and Justice for all." In its present text (established by Congress in 1954), it reads: "I pledge allegiance to the flag of the United States of America and to the Republic for which it stands, one nation under God, indivisible, with liberty and justice for all."

In what year did the Supreme Court decide that it was unconstitutional to require recitation of the Pledge of Allegiance?
Not in the 1960s but in 1943, in the midst of World War II. In that year, the Supreme Court struck down a West Virginia law requiring recitation of the pledge.

What beautiful things are named in the first lines of each stanza of "America the Beautiful"?
There are four stanzas in the song by Katharine Lee Bates (1850–1929), originally published in 1895 and revised in 1904 and 1911. The stanzas begin respectively with these lines:

1. O beautiful for spacious skies
2. O beautiful for pilgrim feet
3. O beautiful for heroes proved
4. O beautiful for patriot dream

What does Flag Day commemorate?
Instituted in 1897 and celebrated on June 14, Flag Day marks the day in 1777 that the Continental Congress adopted the "Stars and Stripes" as the American flag.

What was the nation's first national monument?
The Devil's Tower, Wyoming, established by President Theodore Roosevelt in 1906.

For whom is Mount Rushmore named?
The granite-laden mountain is said to be named for 19th-century New York attorney Charles E. Rushmore. Legend holds that while Rushmore was visiting the Black Hills on business related to his mining clients, he asked the name of a nearby mountain. One member of his group joked, "Why, that is Mount Rushmore," and the name stuck.

Who carved the faces on Mount Rushmore?
Idaho-born sculptor Gutzon Borglum (1867–1941), with the help of his son, from 1927 to 1941. The faces are those of Thomas Jefferson, Abraham Lincoln, Theodore Roosevelt, and George Washington.

Where can you find Edison's last breath?
A vial containing the air representing Thomas Alva Edison's last exhalation is a prime draw at the Henry Ford Museum in Dearborn, Michigan. Originally known as the Edison Institute for Technology in honor of Ford's inventor friend, the museum also includes a slab of concrete with Edison's footprints in addition to more general Americana like antique cars, steam trains, and a McDonald's arch.

When was the moving electric sign installed around the New York Times building?
The electric sign on 1 Times Square at 42nd Street that displays headlines was installed in 1928. At that time, the building housed offices of the *New York Times* and was known as the Times Tower. It is now owned by several general and limited partners and runs headlines from *New York Newsday*. Main offices for the *New York Times* are located on 43rd Street, in the building originally meant to be an annex to the Times Tower.

What was the tallest building in the world before the Empire State Building was opened?

From 1929 to 1931, it was the Chrysler Building in New York City. In the 1920s, its architect, William Van Alen, was commissioned to design the world's tallest building. Simultaneously his former partner, H. Craig Severance, was commissioned by another company to do the same. A competition ensued and it appeared that Severance's design for the Bank of Manhattan Company in New York would better Van Alen's design by two feet. However, when workers secretly added the spire to the Chrysler Building, it reached a record-breaking 1,046 feet. On May 1, 1931, the new 1,250-foot Empire State Building surpassed them both.

How long is the boardwalk in Atlantic City?
The 60-foot-wide wood, steel, and concrete structure is about 4½ miles long. It continues on another two miles into Ventnor City, south of Atlantic City. The first boardwalk in Atlantic City was built in 1870.

What is the difference between Hoover Dam and Boulder Dam?
There is none. Both are names for the same dam, erected in 1931–36 on the Colorado River between Nevada and Arizona. The dam is over 700 feet high and 1,200 feet long.

At the 1939 New York World's Fair, how large were the Trylon and the Perisphere?
The symbols of the theme of the fair, "The World of Tomorrow," were massive: The Trylon, a tapering three-sided shaft, was 750 feet high; the Perisphere was a globe 200 feet in diameter. The two objects were built at a cost of $1.7 million.

For what World's Fair was the Space Needle in Seattle erected?
The 600-foot futuristic steel structure was erected for the Century 21 exposition in 1962.

How long did passengers use New York's original Pennsylvania Station?
For 53 years, from its opening in 1910 to its demolition in 1963. Designed by McKim, Mead & White, the two-square-block structure was made of granite with a Doric colonnade. It was torn down to make way for the Madison Square Garden sports and office complex.

Which part of the National Gallery of Art in Washington, D.C., is the work of architect I. M. Pei?
The East Wing, built in 1978.

What zoos in the United States receive the most visitors?
In 1990, the U.S. zoos with highest attendance were:

1. Lincoln Park Zoo, Chicago, Illinois
2. San Diego Zoo, California
3. National Zoo, Washington, D.C.
4. Busch Gardens, Tampa, Florida
5. St. Louis Zoo, Missouri

When were the words "Pan Am" removed from the Pan Am Building in New York City?
In 1992, the words "Pan Am" were replaced by "MetLife" on the crown of the building at 200 Park Avenue. The change marked the final end of Pan American World Airways, which ceased operations in December 1991 but had housed offices in the building. It was also more accurate, since Metropolitan Life Insurance Company had been the building's owner since 1981. The white neon MetLife sign was officially lit on January 13, 1993, thirty years after the Pan Am building was erected in 1963.

Law and Order

Who was the first person executed for witchcraft in America?
Margaret Jones of Charlestown, Massachusetts, on June 15, 1648—nearly five decades before the Salem witch trials of 1692–93.

How many people were killed in the Salem witch trials?
The series of trials in Massachusetts in 1692–93 resulted in 27 convictions. Of those, 20 were executed: 19 were hanged, one was crushed to death. In 1693, Massachusetts governor William Phips created a new court, with stricter guidelines for evidence. Through it, remaining prisoners were either acquitted or set free.

Who was John Peter Zenger's attorney during Zenger's trial for seditious libel?
Philadelphia lawyer Andrew Hamilton (c. 1676–1741), born in Scotland, successfully defended the German-born editor's right to print true accusations against the colonial governor of New York. The famous trial in 1735 was a landmark for freedom of the press.

When was the first meeting of the Supreme Court?
February 2, 1790, in New York City. John Jay presided as the first Chief Justice of the Supreme Court from 1789 to 1795.

How many chief justices of the Supreme Court have there been?
Sixteen, beginning with John Jay and running through William H. Rehnquist, who joined the court as an associate in 1972 and became chief justice in 1986.

Who killed Billy the Kid?
William H. Bonney (1859–81), the New York-born symbol of the outlaw West, was shot dead by Sheriff Pat Garrett. Barely into his twenties, Bonney had become infamous as a cattle rustler in frontier New Mexico.

Who killed Jesse James?
The bank robber was shot in the back of the head by his reward-seeking cousin, Robert Ford, on April 3, 1882. James was 34.

How long did it take Sacco and Vanzetti to move from arrest to execution?
It took seven years, from their arrest in May 1920 to their electrocution on August 23, 1927. The Italian-born anarchists Nicola Sacco and Bartolomeo Vanzetti were convicted of robbery and murder in South Braintree, Massachusetts. The evidence was shaky and the conviction seemed motivated by ethnic and political bias. In 1977, Massachusetts governor Michael Dukakis pardoned Sacco and Vanzetti posthumously.

What did Al Capone name as his profession?
The gangster's business cards said he was a second-hand furniture dealer in Chicago.

What was known as the "Noble Experiment"?
Prohibition of the manufacture and sale of liquor, which was put into effect by the 18th Amendment in 1920 and lasted until repeal by the 21st Amendment in 1933.

When was the FBI Identification Division founded?
The division of the Federal Bureau of Investigation that maintains the world's largest fingerprint files was founded in 1924. The FBI itself was founded in 1908.

Who won the Scopes trial?
The State of Tennessee, represented by prosecutor William Jennings Bryan, won its 1925 case against John Thomas Scopes, a high-school biology teacher charged with illegally teaching the theory of evolution. Despite the efforts of defense attorney Clarence Darrow, Scopes was convicted and fined $100. However, an appeals court voided the fine on a technicality: a jury was required for fines over $50. The Tennessee law prohibiting the teaching of evolution stayed on the books until 1967.

How much was stolen in the Brink's robbery of 1950?
Eleven men stole $2.5 million in cash, checks, and securities from the headquarters of the Brink's armored car company. The crime took place in Boston, Massachusetts, on January 17, 1950. After several years undercover, one of the robbers confessed to the police, and eight of the 11 men were eventually sentenced to life in prison.

Where in New York City did the attack on Kitty Genovese occur?
Bar manager Catherine Genovese was stabbed to death in Kew Gardens, Queens, in the early morning hours of March 13, 1964. Her neighbors looked on from their windows but ignored her calls for help. The case became a paradigm for urban lawlessness and apathy.

What nationality was Sirhan Sirhan, the assassin of Robert Kennedy?
He was a Jordanian-born American. He shot Kennedy, then a

candidate for the Democratic presidential nomination, on June 5, 1968.

Where was James Earl Ray arrested?
The assassin of civil rights leader Martin Luther King was arrested by Scotland Yard detectives at a London airport on June 8, 1968. Ray had shot King on April 4.

How soon after coming to office did President Gerald Ford pardon Richard Nixon?
Ford pardoned his predecessor on September 8, 1974, 30 days after coming to office on August 9. The unconditional pardon exonerated Nixon of any crimes he might have committed as president.

When did crack first appear in the U.S.?
The inexpensive, crystallized cocaine was first noted in urban areas on the west coast in 1983.

When was Mafia boss Paul Castellano killed?
The 71-year-old head of the Gambino crime family was shot dead on December 16, 1985, on 46th Street near Third Avenue in New York City. His successor, John Gotti, reputedly masterminded the killing.

Which Supreme Court Justice served the longest term?
William O. Douglas (1898–1980), who served 36 years (1939–75). Four justices served 34 years: John Marshall (1801–35); Stephen J. Field (1863–97); Hugo L. Black (1937–71); and William J. Brennan, Jr. (1956–90).

When was the Supreme Court first called the "Nine Old Men"?
They received the disparaging epithet when they opposed President Franklin Roosevelt's reforms during the Great Depression.

The Nine Old Men was the title of a 1936 book on the Supreme Court by Drew Pearson and Robert S. Allen.

How much prison time did Oliver North serve?
None. The Marine colonel at the center of the Iran-Contra scandal was convicted in 1989 of falsifying and destroying records, accepting an illegal gratuity, and obstructing Congress, but was not given prison time. Instead, he was given a three-year suspended sentence and ordered to perform 1,200 hours of community service. In 1990, a U.S. Court of Appeals panel overturned his conviction.

How much time passed between Amy Fisher's shooting of Mary Jo Buttafuoco and the premiere of the TV-movies on the subject?
Less than eight months had gone by when the three network television movies on the "Long Island Lolita" shooting aired. The teenaged Fisher shot Buttafuoco, wife of her alleged lover Joey, on May 19, 1992, in Massapequa, Long Island. The NBC, CBS, and ABC TV-movies aired in the week from December 28, 1992, to January 3, 1993. All three earned high ratings.

Military History

Who was the Jenkins behind the War of Jenkins's Ear?
Robert Jenkins was a British sailor smuggling slaves to the Spanish colonies in defiance of the Spanish trade monopoly. A Spanish captain caught Jenkins and cut off one of his ears. Jenkins was displayed in the House of Commons by people seeking to ignite a war with Spain. The war that followed from 1739 to 1743 was called the War of Jenkins's Ear.

How many French and Indian Wars were there? What were they called in England?
Four major "French and Indian Wars" were fought in colonial times by Britain and France for control of North America. Each was part of a larger struggle involving shifting alliances, fighting in Europe, and colonial battles in other parts of the world. The struggle ended in 1763 with Britain winning most of France's American empire, including Canada and territories east of the Mississippi River. The four wars were:

American Name	European Name
King William's War (1689–97)	The War of the Grand Alliance
Queen Anne's War (1701–13)	The War of the Spanish Succession
King George's War (1744–48)	The War of the Austrian Succession

The French and Indian War   The Seven Years' War
(1754–63)

Who killed who in the Deerfield Massacre?
A company of French and Caughnawaga Indians killed about 50 of the 300 residents of the English colonial village of Deerfield, Massachusetts, in a predawn raid on February 29, 1704, during Queen Anne's War. Almost 100 settlers were taken to Canada as prisoners.

Did both Wolfe and Montcalm die on the battlefield in the Battle of Quebec?
The British general James Wolfe was killed on the battlefield during the engagement on September 13, 1759, but the French general Louis Joseph, Marquis de Montcalm, was only wounded. He died in bed early the next morning. On September 18, Quebec, the capital of New France, surrendered to the British, marking a crucial turning point in the French and Indian War.

Where was Fort William Henry?
The British fort, captured by the French in 1757 during the French and Indian War, was located in New York near Lake George.

Where was Fort McHenry?
The fort that withstood British bombardment during the War of 1812 was on the Patapsco River in Baltimore, Maryland.

Where was Fort Henry?
The Confederate stronghold captured by the Union in 1862 was on the Tennessee River in Tennessee.

Was it a "Shay" or a "Shays" who led the rebellion of 1786?
Shays's Rebellion (with the apostrophe *after* Shays) was named for army veteran Daniel Shays, who led an uprising against the

Massachusetts state government in 1786. This action was one of a series of protests in 1786–87 by American farmers and workers throughout the young nation against state and local enforcement of tax collection and judgments for debt. Shays's particular uprising was crushed by the state militia under General Benjamin Lincoln.

What kind of whiskey was involved in the Whiskey Rebellion?

Whiskey distilled from surplus corn was at the heart of this 1794 rebellion by western Pennsylvania farmers. The farmers refused to pay a federal excise tax on whiskey, which was easier to store and transport than corn and was even used as currency. President George Washington stopped the rebellion with a force of 13,000 militiamen. The tax itself was repealed once Thomas Jefferson took office as president in 1801.

Where is Tippecanoe?

In Indiana. In 1811, William Henry Harrison led a regiment to victory over Indians, led by Tecumseh. Harrison was elected president (with running mate John Tyler) in 1840, using the slogan "Tippecanoe and Tyler Too!"

Did the U.S. ever attack Canada?

Yes. The U.S. attempted to conquer Canada, then a British colony, in 1813, during the War of 1812. American forces got as far as burning the city of York (now Toronto) before being turned back. In retribution, the British burned much of Washington, D.C., the following year.

Where in Texas did William Travis, commander of the Alamo, come from?

Travis was not from Texas but from South Carolina. A lawyer and lieutenant-colonel, Travis was one of many Southerners who responded to Texas's call for volunteers to help in their revolution against Mexico, which began in 1835. (Southerners sympathized with the rebels because the province of Texas was a slave-owning territory mostly settled by Southerners.) Travis led the group of Texans and allies who made a stand against Mexican forces at the Alamo, a fortified mission in San Antonio.

How many defenders died at the Alamo?
Every soldier defending the fort (about 182 in all) died in the fighting on March 6, 1836, or were killed as prisoners soon after. The dead included Travis, knife-inventor James Bowie, and frontiersman and former U.S. Congressman Davy Crockett.

When did the United States first conquer a foreign capital?
On September 14, 1847, during the Mexican War, U.S. troops under the command of General Winfield Scott occupied Mexico City. Mexico made peace with the U.S. in 1848.

How long did it take for news of Custer's last stand to be published in the press?
Eleven days. The massacre of George Armstrong Custer and his Seventh Cavalry by the Sioux Indians took place on June 25, 1876, on the Little Big Horn River in Montana Territory. The news was first published by the *Bozeman Times* in Bozeman, Montana, on July 6, 1876—two days after the nation celebrated its centennial. The *Times* got its story from a cavalry scout named H. M. Taylor.

What military action was known as "that splendid little war"?
The Spanish-American War was so called by then U.S. Secretary of State John Hays.

What was "embalmed beef"?
It was a nickname for the tinned meat fed to troops at training camps during the Spanish-American War. The meat gained its

nickname because it caused diseases such as typhoid fever, dysentery, and food poisoning, which eventually claimed thousands of soldiers' lives.

In what war did the phrase "meatless Mondays" originate?
World War I. Herbert Hoover, director of the Food Administration, urged Americans to observe "meatless Mondays" and "wheatless Wednesdays" to conserve food for the war.

What action by Pancho Villa spurred the U.S. to invade Mexico in 1916?
In 1916, the rebel leader raided Columbus, New Mexico, and killed 18 people. Villa opposed U.S. influence in Mexico and was seeking to overthrow the Mexican government. In response, President Woodrow Wilson sent General John Pershing and 6,000 troops into northern Mexico on a mission to find Villa. Pershing's expedition clashed with Mexican troops but never caught up with Villa.

How many Americans served in the armed forces during the first and second world wars?
About 4.7 million served in World War I. Over three times as many—16.1 million—served in World War II.

How many American lives were lost in World War I?
The total death count was 116,516, including 53,402 deaths in battle and 63,114 from other causes, mostly disease. An additional 204,002 soldiers received nonlethal wounds.

How does that compare to World War II casualties?
In World War II, over three times as many Americans died: 405,399, including 291,557 in battle and 113,842 from other causes. An additional 670,846 Americans received nonlethal wounds.

How many Germans did Sergeant Alvin York capture single-handedly in World War I?
The hero of the Meuse-Argonne offensive, launched on September 26, 1918, killed 25 Germans and captured 132, along with 35 machine guns. The Tennessee sharpshooter, who had petitioned unsuccessfully for exemption as a conscientious objector, was lionized for his exploits and awarded the Congressional Medal of Honor and the French Croix de Guerre.

Who were the "Big Four" who negotiated peace at Versailles at the end of World War I?
The Allied leaders who forced Germany to accept the Versailles Treaty of 1919 were:

Woodrow Wilson (U.S.)
Georges Clemenceau (France)
David Lloyd George (Great Britain)
Vittorio Orlando (Italy)

What does the military nickname "G.I." stand for?
Government Issue. The term was introduced during World War II.

When was the draft age of U.S. recruits set at 18?
The government lowered it from 20 to 18 on November 12, 1942, to expand American forces during World War II.

When did the draft end in the U.S.?
On January 27, 1973, after years of antidraft protests. The end of the draft coincided with a ceasefire that stopped direct involvement of U.S. ground forces in hostilities in Vietnam.

What did the G.I. Bill do?
Officially known as the Servicemen's Readjustment Act of 1944, the G.I. Bill gave a variety of benefits to World War II veterans. The benefits included medical care in veterans' hospitals, low-

interest mortgages, grants for higher education, unemployment compensation, and vocational rehabilitation.

What was the latitude of the boundary between North and South Korea that the U.S. was defending in the Korean War (1950–53)?
The 38th parallel.

Who replaced General Douglas MacArthur when he was fired by President Harry S. Truman during the Korean War?
General Matthew B. Ridgway replaced MacArthur as commander of U.N. forces in South Korea. Truman removed MacArthur from command on April 11, 1951, for publicly criticizing Truman's policy of limiting the war to the Korean peninsula.

How many times was Seoul occupied by the North Koreans during the Korean War?
Twice. The capital of South Korea fell to invaders from North Korea in June 1950, inciting President Harry Truman to commit American troops as part of United Nations forces sent to repel the invasion. U.N. forces recaptured Seoul on September 26, only to be forced out when Communist China entered the war and recaptured Seoul in January 1951. The U.N. forces retook Seoul on March 14.

Under which president were the first U.S. military advisors sent to South Vietnam?
Dwight D. Eisenhower (served 1953–61).

How many members of Congress voted against the Gulf of Tonkin Resolution?
The 1964 resolution that gave President Johnson the right to use extensive military force in southeast Asia was approved by all of the House of Representatives and all but two members of the

Senate. The two dissenting senators were Wayne Morse of Oregon and Ernest Gruening of Alaska.

What U.S. ships were fired on in the Gulf of Tonkin in August 1964?

None. The U.S. Navy reported that month that the USS *Maddox* and the USS *Turner* had been fired upon by three North Vietnamese patrol boats. Later investigations showed no evidence of any such attacks.

What did "ARVN" stand for in the Vietnam War?

The Army of the Republic of Viet Nam, the army that South Vietnam fielded against North Vietnam.

Who won the Tet Offensive?

The Tet Offensive was a general attack in January 1968 by North Vietnamese forces against South Vietnamese cities. Militarily, North Vietnam lost since they suffered heavy losses and failed to hold any city. But strategically North Vietnam delivered a severe blow to the U.S. by showing that the war was far from over and undermining domestic support.

Under what president did the last American troops leave Vietnam?

Gerald Ford (served 1974–77). The troops left on April 29, 1975. The Saigon government surrendered shortly thereafter.

What went wrong with President Jimmy Carter's military attempt to free the hostages in Iran?

Carter had authorized a commando raid to free the American hostages held in Teheran since November 4, 1979. On the night of April 24, 1980, six U.S. C-130 cargo planes landed in the desert 300 miles southeast of Teheran. In the midst of a blinding sandstorm, three of the operation's eight helicopters malfunctioned. The mission came to a fiery end when one of the helicopters crashed into a cargo plane. Eight soldiers were killed, five were severely burned, and seven aircraft were destroyed. The hostages were not freed until Carter left office on January 20, 1981.

How high were military expenditures during Reagan's first term?
They totalled $1.5 trillion dollars. Between 1981 and 1986, the national debt doubled, expanding from $1 trillion to $2 trillion.

How many U.S. and Iraqi troops were involved in the Gulf War?
The U.S. fielded about 540,000 troops, by far the most of any nation in the coalition it led against Iraq. Iraqi ground forces in the Kuwaiti theater of operations were estimated at 545,000.

How many casualties did each nation suffer?
In the brief conflict from January to March 1991, the U.S. suffered 148 combat deaths and 213 wounded. The number of Iraqi combat deaths, according to a Saudi Arabian estimate, was 80,000 to 100,000, though the exact figure is not known.

What were General H. Norman Schwarzkopf's qualifications for command of the allied operation against Iraq?
A veteran of Vietnam and Grenada and head of the U.S. Central Command, Schwarzkopf had been revising contingency plans for war in the Mideast when Iraq invaded Kuwait on August 2, 1990. Having just completed a command-post exercise with Iraq as the mock enemy, Schwarzkopf was prepared to take charge of the real thing. The general retired from the army soon after leading the allied forces to victory.

Who reported that Iraq was left in "near-apocalyptic" conditions after the Gulf War?
A United Nations mission that visited Iraq on March 10–17, 1991, made this report, saying: "the recent conflict has wrought

near-apocalyptic results upon the infrastructure of what had been until January 1991 a rather highly urbanized and mechanized society."

Were there more journalists or troops on the beach when U.S. forces first arrived in Somalia?
Three dozen Navy Seals arrived on the beach at Mogadishu early on December 9, 1992, to begin the famine relief operation. They were outnumbered two to one by more than 75 reporters and camera crew members waiting to cover the story.

Native American History

When did human beings first settle in North America?
The date of the first human migration to the Americas is still in dispute. It may be as early as 35,000 years ago or, according to some archeologists, no more than 12,000 years ago. Whichever date turns out to be correct, it is believed that the first Americans migrated from northeastern Siberia across the Bering Strait, then a land bridge.

What is the oldest confirmed site of human habitation in the continental United States?
It is an archeological site at Clovis, New Mexico, that dates back 11,500 years, to a time when mammoths were still alive. The site was discovered in 1952.

What was Squanto's tribe?
The English-speaking American Indian famous for befriending the Pilgrims at Plymouth colony in the winter of 1620–21 was a Pawtuxet.

What is the difference between a tepee and a wigwam?
The tepee was a conical dwelling made from buffalo hides, supported by poles, and often painted or decorated with beadwork. It was commonly used by Native Americans of the Great Plains.

The wigwam was a rounded dwelling made from woven mats or birch bark over a framework of poles. It was widely used in the Eastern Woodlands.

When did the Great Plains Indians start riding horses?
Not until after 1540, when Spanish explorer Francisco de Coronado, traveling through Kansas, let most of his 260 horses escape. There were no horses in America until the Spanish brought them. The Great Plains Indians tamed the descendants of these horses and made them an integral part of their culture.

What was the first major war against Indians in New England?
The first such conflict was the Pequot War against the Pequot Indians of Connecticut in 1637. In the bloodiest encounter of the war, English colonists burned a Pequot village near Long Island Sound, killing hundreds of Indian men, women, and children.

What did *chinook* mean to an Indian of the Pacific Northwest?
It was a dance to summon the warm wind to melt the snow. It also refers to the wind itself and to the Chinook people of the Columbia River valley. "Chinook jargon" is a pidgin language based on Indian languages, French, and English, formerly spoken in the Pacific Northwest.

How are the Apache and Navajo tribes related?
Native to New Mexico and Arizona, both tribes are members of the Athapascan language family. This language family also includes the Kiowa-Apache of the Southwest and several tribes in Alaska and western Canada.

Which tribe was known to U.S. settlers as the "Cossacks of the Plains"?

This moniker was given to the Comanche, a Shoshonean-speaking people who lived in western Texas, western Oklahoma, and parts of Kansas and New Mexico. Masters of horsemanship and warfare, the Comanche clashed regularly with U.S. settlers until being forced onto reservations in the 1860s and 1870s.

What tribes are related to the Sioux?
Many tribes besides the Sioux speak Siouan languages, including the Biloxi of Mississippi, the Winnebagos of Wisconsin, the Osages of Missouri, and the Omahas of Iowa and Nebraska.

How do you say "Crow" in the Crow language?
The name for this tribe in their own Siouan language is *Absaroke,* meaning "crow, sparrowhawk, or bird people." The French called these people of the Rocky Mountains *gens des corbeaux,* from which the English "Crow" is translated.

What is a sweat lodge?
Common to many American Indian tribes, it is an enclosed steam bath in which steam is produced by pouring cold water over hot stones. Religious ceremonies performed in the sweat lodge are related to spiritual purification and communication with the divine.

Who led the Great Pueblo Revolt of 1680?
Popé, a Pueblo medicine man, planned the Indian revolt against the Spanish in New Mexico. The Pueblos and Apaches took over Santa Fe, drove out or killed Spanish settlers, and forced the Spanish to abandon New Mexico. The Spanish recaptured Santa Fe in 1693; the revolt was not entirely crushed until 1698.

What were the nations of the Iroquois Confederacy?
In the 1500s, they were the Cayuga, Mohawks, Oneida, Onon-

daga, and Seneca. Around 1720, these five nations, based in New York, were joined by another tribe, the Tuscarora.

What was the Iroquois warpath?

Running from the Hudson River to Lake Erie in what is now New York State, the warpath was a trail about a foot wide and six inches deep. The Iroquois traveled single file down this forest path when invading enemy territory.

Who were the Indians of the French and Indian War?

In the struggle between France and England for control of North America (1754–63), most, but not all, Indians fought on the French side. They included the Abnaki of Maine, the Delaware and Shawnee of Pennsylvania, and the Potawatomi and Ottawa of Michigan and Wisconsin. The English relied on the six nations of the Iroquois Confederacy.

Who were the rebels of "Pontiac's Rebellion"?

They were an alliance of American Indian tribes of the Great Lakes region, including the Chippewa, Potawatomi, Huron, Shawnee, Delaware, and Seneca. In 1763, they made war against the British, who had just taken over the territory from the French. The rebellion was mostly defeated by 1764. However, Pontiac, an Ottawa chief who was among their leaders, did not surrender until 1766.

What was the name of the American Indian woman who guided Lewis and Clark?

Sacajawea was the woman who helped Lewis and Clark find their way on their western expedition beginning in 1804. A Shoshoni, she was captured in childhood by the Hidatsa Sioux and sold to the French Canadian Toussaint Charbonneau, who took her as a wife. Charbonneau, a guide and interpreter on the voyage, brought along Sacajawea and their infant child.

What rank did Tecumseh reach in the British army?
The Shawnee political and military leader (1768–1813) fought against the U.S. as a British brigadier-general in the War of 1812. Born in what is now western Ohio, he had resisted U.S. encroachment on Native American lands but was defeated at the Battle of Tippecanoe in 1811. When the War of 1812 broke out, Tecumseh joined the British side and was killed in 1813 at the Battle of the Thames in Ontario.

Who developed the first system of writing in Cherokee?
A Cherokee named Sequoyah finished the system in Arkansas in 1821. Sequoyah neither spoke nor wrote English, but he had an idea of the power of writing: "I thought that would be like catching a wild animal and taming it." His alphabet had a character for each of 86 Cherokee syllables. The system spread quickly among Cherokees across the country.

Who were the "Five Civilized Tribes"?
They were the five southern tribes forced into exile in Oklahoma as a result of the Indian Removal Act of 1830: the Choctaw of Mississippi, the Creek of Alabama, the Cherokee of Georgia, the Chickasaw of Mississippi, and the Seminole of Florida. The act required all Indian tribes east of the Mississippi River, however settled and "civilized," to sell their lands and go west.

What was the "Trail of Tears"?
It refers to the "removal," or forced exile, of 17,000 Cherokee from Georgia in 1838–39, under the terms of the Indian Removal Act of 1830. About 4,000 people—one in four Cherokees—died of hunger and disease on their way to Oklahoma.

What Indian war was fought in the Florida Everglades?
The Seminole War of 1835–42, sparked by the Seminole tribe's refusal to be exiled to Oklahoma. The tribe's greatest hero, Osceola, held off U.S. troops with guerrilla-style actions until his

capture in 1837. He died in prison, but the fighting dragged on for several more years.

Who captured Geronimo?

Geronimo (1829–1909), leader of the Chiricahua Apaches, born in what is now Arizona, repeatedly defied the U.S. Army's attempts to restrict his movements to the San Carlos Reservation in Arizona. He finally surrendered to General Nelson Miles in Skeleton County, Arizona, on September 4, 1886. He spent the rest of his life in captivity.

What is a Ghost Dance?

A ceremonial spiritual dance related to the teachings of Wovoka, a Paiute medicine man of Nevada who foresaw the restoration of the American continent to the Indians. Wovoka's revolutionary message, preached in the late 1880s, provoked repression from U.S. officials, culminating in the Battle of Wounded Knee in 1890.

What was the last major battle between U.S. troops and Native Americans?

The Battle of Wounded Knee, South Dakota, on December 29, 1890. Twenty-nine U.S. soldiers and nearly 200 Sioux men, women, and children were killed.

Who was Carlos Montezuma?

A Yavapai from Arizona, Carlos Montezuma (1865–1923) was a physician who became a prominent advocate for Native Americans. In his newsletter *Wassaja* and elsewhere, he spoke out for Indian rights. He helped to found the Society of American Indians in 1911.

What organization led the 1973 takeover of Wounded Knee, South Dakota?

Members of the American Indian Movement (AIM) led about 200 Sioux in the 70-day occupation of the town, site of the 1890 battle. AIM demanded redress of American Indians' grievances against the federal government.

What state does Ben Nighthorse Campbell represent?
The Native American senator, whose term began in 1993, represents Colorado. He is a member of the Northern Cheyenne tribe of Montana.

Omnibus

When was the phrase "rub out" first used to mean "kill"?
The phrase first appeared not among gangsters in the Roaring '20s but among the rugged fur traders and trappers of the Great Plains and Rocky Mountains in the early 19th century. It came into more widespread use in World War I.

What is the most common initial letter for U.S. states?
"M" and "N" are tied with eight states each:

Maine	Nebraska
Maryland	Nevada
Massachusetts	New Hampshire
Michigan	New Jersey
Minnesota	New Mexico
Mississippi	New York
Missouri	North Carolina
Montana	North Dakota

What is the root of the American word "buckaroo"?
It comes from the Spanish *vaquero*, meaning cowboy. It was picked up as Americans moved into western lands once owned by Mexico.

In what colony did the "Peggy Stewart Tea Party" take place?
In Maryland. The burning of the tea ship *Peggy Stewart* was in-

spired by the Boston Tea Party of December 16, 1773. Like its more famous counterpart, this act of destruction was committed to protest British duties on tea and the monopoly of the British East India Company.

Where are the following forts located?
    Fort Necessity—Pennsylvania
    Fort Duquesne—Pittsburgh, Pennsylvania
    Fort Ticonderoga—New York State
    Fort Laramie—Wyoming
    Fort Sumter—Charleston, South Carolina
    Fort Corregidor—Manila Bay, Philippines

Who wrote *The American Crisis?*
The sequence of 16 pamphlets, published 1776–83, was written by Revolutionary War patriot Thomas Paine.

Who wrote The Present Crisis?
The anti-slavery poem was written in 1844 by Massachusetts poet James Russell Lowell.

Who wrote Six Crises?
The 1962 memoir was written by former vice-president and future president Richard Nixon.

What kind of rockets glared redly in "The Star-Spangled Banner"?
The rockets that the national anthem refers to were Congreve rockets, invented by Sir Thomas Congreve and used by the British in the War of 1812. The noisy, hissing missiles, 42 inches long, were used throughout the British campaigns in Maryland in 1813–14. The rockets initially terrified the Americans but proved to be ineffective, killing only two men in combat and doing little property damage.

Did Abraham Lincoln write the Gettysburg Address on the back of an envelope?
No. Judging from the many drafts of the speech that have been discovered, the speech was fashioned through the traditional method of writing and revising. It was presented on November 19, 1863, at the dedication of the national cemetery at Gettysburg, four months after the Battle of Gettysburg.

Where can you find the original copy of Lincoln's Gettysburg Address?
In the Library of Congress.

What is the meaning of the letters D or P on American coins?
They are mint marks, indicating the city in which the coin is pressed. The letter D indicates that the coin was made in Denver; P denotes Philadelphia. Pennies no longer carry mint marks.

When did the last veteran of the American Revolution die?
1867.

To what war did Decoration Day pay homage?
The holiday, which was first widely celebrated on May 30, 1868, was originally meant to remind citizens to decorate with wreaths the graves of soldiers killed in the Civil War. The holiday has since been renamed Memorial Day and is observed on the last Monday in May to honor the dead of all American wars.

How highly ranked was World War II general Douglas MacArthur in his graduating class at West Point?
He was ranked first of 93 in the class of 1903.

How highly ranked was Civil War officer George Armstrong Custer?
He was 35th of 35 in the class of 1861.

What did the World's Columbian Exposition of 1893 celebrate?
Formally conceived to celebrate the 400th anniversary of Columbus's discovery of America, the Exposition in Chicago also served to establish Chicago as a cosmopolitan international urban center. To plan the Exposition, several of the nation's top urban planners were recruited, including Daniel Burnham and Frederick Law Olmsted. Founder of *Poetry* magazine Harriet Monroe was commissioned to write a poem of dedication. The Exposition, which ran from May through October 1893, attracted millions of visitors from several continents.

To what fair does the song "Meet Me in St. Louis" refer?
The song by Andrew B. Sterling and Kerry Mills refers to the 1904 Louisiana Purchase Exposition in St. Louis, Missouri. The tune provides the leitmotif for the 1944 musical film *Meet Me in St. Louis,* starring Judy Garland, about a St. Louis family faced with a move to New York just as the 1904 Exposition is about to open.

In what American cities were the following world's fairs held?
   1876—Centennial Exposition—Philadelphia
   1901—Pan-American Exposition—Buffalo, New York
   1905—Lewis and Clark Centennial Exposition—Portland, Oregon
   1926—Sesquicentennial Exposition—Philadelphia
   1933–34—Century of Progress International Exposition—Chicago
   1935—California Pacific International Exposition—San Diego
   1939–40—New York World's Fair—New York City
   1939–40—Golden Gate International Exposition—Treasure Island, San Francisco
   1962—Century 21 Exposition—Seattle
   1964–65—New York World's Fair—New York City
   1974—Expo '74—Spokane, Washington

1982—World's Fair—Knoxville, Tennessee
1984—Louisiana World Exposition—New Orleans

Did Sigmund Freud ever visit the U.S.?

The Viennese founder of psychoanalysis visited the U.S. only once, to receive an honorary doctor of law degree from Clark University, Worcester, Massachusetts, in 1909. Freud got sick eating American food and was unimpressed by U.S. culture. He later said, "Yes, America is gigantic, but a gigantic mistake."

When did the passenger pigeon become extinct?

Once common in U.S. skies and hunted widely as cheap food, the last known passenger pigeon died in the Cincinnati Zoo on September 1, 1914.

What was *The Negro Motorist Green Book*?

Started in 1936, it was a travel guide designed to "give the Negro traveler information that will keep him from running into difficulties, embarrassments, and to make his trips more enjoyable."

What is "sittin' in the catbird seat"?

Popularized by baseball announcer Red Barber, it means sitting pretty or being in an enviable position. The Mississippi-born Barber used this 19th-century Southern expression while announcing games for the Brooklyn Dodgers in the 1940s and 1950s, and in the 1950s and 1960s for the New York Yankees. A catbird is the common name for the North American thrush (*Dumetella carolinensis*), whose cry resembles a cat's meow.

What are the middle names of the following Presidents?

Dwight D. Eisenhower—David
Gerald R. Ford—Rudolph
James A. Garfield—Abram
Ulysses S. Grant—Simpson
Warren G. Harding—Gamaliel

Rutherford B. Hayes—Birchard
James K. Polk—Knox
Ronald W. Reagan—Wilson

What was a U-2?
It was an American high-altitude reconnaissance plane. The plane became infamous when a U-2 flown by Francis Gary Powers was shot down over the Soviet Union on May 1, 1960, sparking an international incident.

How much does a B-2 bomber cost?
At about $865 million each, the radar-evading "Stealth" strategic bomber built by Northrop for the U.S. Air Force is considered the most expensive weapons system in American history.

When was the first Earth Day in the U.S.?
Sponsored by a nonprofit youth organization called Environmental Action, Inc., Earth Day was first celebrated on April 20, 1970, to draw attention to the pollution of the nation's environment. The nationwide action involved more than 2,000 college campuses, 2,000 community groups, and 10,000 schools. Over 20 U.S. Senators spoke against pollution. Earth Day continues to be marked by environmentalists.

When did President Nixon introduce the term the "Silent Majority"?
He first mentioned it in a speech about the Vietnam War in November 1969. He used the term to refer to Americans who quietly supported his policies and practices in contrast to his vocal opposition.

What Republican speechwriter described the press as "nattering nabobs of negativism"?
William Safire wrote the phrase for Vice-President Spiro Agnew in 1970.

Who came up with "pusillanimous pussyfooters"?
Agnew speechwriter Pat Buchanan, also in 1970.

Who coined the term "POSSLQ"?
The term, which refers to "Persons of Opposite Sex Sharing Living Quarters," was coined in the 1970s by the U.S. Census Bureau in response to the tripling of the number of unmarried persons sharing households between 1970 and 1980.

Who coined the term "conspicuous consumption"?
Thorstein Veblen in *The Theory of the Leisure Class* (1899). Veblen used the term to excoriate Americans who spent lavishly in trying to impress others with their wealth.

Who first used the word "yuppie" in print?
Newspaper columnist Bob Greene is credited with first writing the term in a column in March 1983. The derisive term for "young urban professionals" became widespread by 1984.

What state has produced the most Miss America winners?
Ohio and California are tied with six each.

What state has produced the fewest?
Twenty-three states have produced none at all, even though the Miss America pageant has been crowning beauty queens for over 70 years (since 1921). As of 1993, Alaska, Delaware, Idaho, Maryland, and Wyoming are among the states waiting for recognition.

Personalities

Who was called "Captain Shrimp"?
The undersized Miles Standish was given this nickname by fellow colonist Thomas Morton. Standish (c. 1584–1656) was the military leader of the Plymouth Colony, founded in Massachusetts in 1620. Morton (c. 1590–c. 1647), leader of the rival colony of Merrymount, ridiculed the austere habits and strict religious beliefs of his Pilgrim neighbors.

What was Governor Henry Sloughter's role in colonial history?
The royal governor of New York with the murderous name was responsible for hanging Jacob Leisler in 1691. Leisler was a New York City wine merchant who led a rebellion against royal rule in 1689. As acting governor, Leisler set up an assembly and reformed tax laws until the new governor, Sloughter, stopped him.

Who was Johnson of the Mohawks?
William Johnson (1715–74) was an Irishman who settled in the Mohawk Valley of New York in 1738, at the age of 23. He became a wealthy landowner and trader and treated his Mohawk neighbors with fairness and respect. The Mohawks adopted him as a blood brother, and he took a Mohawk wife, Molly Brant. Johnson's influence helped keep the Iroquois on the British side

during the French and Indian War. He led a combined force of colonists and Mohawks to victory against the French at Lake George in 1755.

Who came first, Daniel Boone or Davy Crockett?

Legendary frontiersman Daniel Boone was an old man when Davy Crockett was just starting his own career as a backwoodsman. Born in Pennsylvania, Boone (1734–1820) is best known for his exploration and settlement of Kentucky. Crockett (1786–1836) served as a U.S. representative from Tennessee and died defending the Alamo. Both men are remembered in folklore for hunting fierce animals, blazing trails, and doing battle with American Indians.

How were Samuel, John, and John Quincy Adams related?

American Revolutionary patriots Samuel (1722–1803) and John Adams (1735–1826) were cousins. John Quincy Adams (1767–1848) was John's son. Two of these men served as president of the U.S.: John (served 1797–1801) and John Quincy (served 1825–29).

Who was the "Hair Buyer of Detroit"?

He was Henry Hamilton, the Detroit settlement's British governor during the American Revolution. To fight the spread of U.S. settlements, he armed massive numbers of Native Americans with knives and ordered them to scalp frontier dwellers.

Who was Publius?

This was the pen name of the authors of *The Federalist Papers* (1787–88)—Alexander Hamilton, James Madison, and John Jay.

Where was the duel between Vice-President Aaron Burr and Alexander Hamilton?

The duel in which Burr shot Hamilton was held on July 11, 1804, in Weehawken, New Jersey. Burr had challenged Hamilton to the duel in response to Hamilton's attacks on his character during the election campaign for governor of New York. Wounded by Burr's pistol, Hamilton died the next day.

Who is the only U.S. president known to have killed a man in a duel?
Andrew Jackson (served 1829–37), who shot and killed Nashville lawyer Charles Dickinson in 1806. The duel resulted from Dickinson's impugning of the honor of Jackson's wife, Rachel Donelson Robards Jackson.

Who was the "Smith" behind Smith College?
Sophia Smith (1796–1870) founded the college for women. After receiving an inheritance upon the death of her brother, a wealthy stockbroker, she was advised by a clergyman to use the money to begin an institution of higher education for women. Plans were drawn up in 1868, and in 1871, Smith College was founded.

Under what pen name did telegraph inventor Samuel F. B. Morse write?
Known as an artist and writer as well as an inventor, Morse wrote a series of highly popular newspaper articles denouncing the immigration of Catholics to the U.S. These were published under the pen name "Brutus." Gathered into book form in 1835, they helped create an American tradition of anti-immigration sentiment.

What politician was known as "The Little Giant"?
Stephen A. Douglas (1813–61), the short but politically powerful congressman from Illinois. A Democrat, he represented Illinois in the House of Representatives (1843–47) and the Senate (1847–61). He lost the 1860 presidential election to Abraham Lincoln.

On what project was the legendary John Henry supposed to have worked?

According to folklore, John Henry was an ex-slave who worked as a steel driver helping to blast the Big Bend Tunnel through the Allegheny Mountains for the Chesapeake and Ohio Railroad in West Virginia in the 1870s. His job was to hammer steel into rock to make holes for explosive charges. In the folk song "The Ballad of John Henry," he matched his strength against a mechanical steam drill. He won the competition but died in the process.

When did Andrew Carnegie present his "Gospel of Wealth"?
In an 1889 speech, the 54-year old steel baron and philanthropist outlined his "Gospel," a set of principles for amassing and sharing wealth. He wrote, "[T]he millionaire will be but a trustee for the poor; entrusted for a season with a great part of the increased wealth of the community, but administering it for the community far better than it could or would have done for itself."

How many times did Eugene Debs run for president?
A labor organizer who led the Pullman strike of 1894, Debs ran for president five times—once in 1900 on the Social Democratic ticket and four times as the Socialist candidate (1904, 1908, 1912, and 1920).

Was Humphrey Bogart ever in combat?
The movie actor (1899–1957) was a veteran of World War I. While serving in the Navy, Bogart was wounded in the shelling of the ship *Leviathan*. The injury resulted in the scarred and partially paralyzed upper lip that gave him his trademark lisp and tight-set mouth.

Who was the "Sage of Baltimore"?
Editor and writer H. L. Mencken (1880–1956), who lived his entire life in Baltimore and wrote for the *Baltimore Sun* for 40 years. His works include *Prejudices* (1919–27) and *The American Language* (1919).

For whom is Duke University named?
Founded in 1838 as the Union Institute and Randolph College, and renamed Trinity College in 1851, the Durham, North Carolina, institution became Duke University in 1924 in commemoration of a $40 million donation from tobacco mogul James B. Duke.

What university did John D. Rockefeller found?
The man (1839–1937) who set up the Standard Oil Trust also founded the University of Chicago.

What university did John D. Rockefeller, Jr., found?
The son (1874–1960) of John D. Rockefeller founded Rockefeller University in New York.

Where did Charles Lindbergh begin his flight across the Atlantic Ocean?
Lindbergh launched *The Spirit of St. Louis* from Roosevelt Field, Long Island, on May 20, 1927, becoming the first person to fly solo across the Atlantic.

Where did he land?
At Le Bourget Field outside Paris, on May 21.

How much money did Charles Lindbergh receive for flying nonstop from New York to Paris?
By crossing the Atlantic on May 20–21, 1927, he won the $25,000 award offered by a New York hotel owner.

How long was Huey Long governor of Louisiana?
The colorful, demagogic Long (1893–1935), nicknamed the "Kingfish," governed Louisiana from 1928 to 1932, when he resigned to enter the U.S. Senate.

How long was he a U.S. senator?
Elected in 1930, he deferred his entry into the Senate until 1932. He stayed there until he was killed by an assassin's bullet in 1935. His wife finished his term.

How tall was Fiorello La Guardia?

The Republican mayor of New York City (1934–45), known as the "Little Flower," was five feet two inches tall.

Who was the 12-year-old "baby vet" who fought at Guadalcanal?

Calvin L. Graham (1930–92), born in Canton, Texas, was the boy who lied about his age so he could enlist in the U.S. Navy at age 12 during World War II. Wounded by shrapnel during the Battle of Guadalcanal in 1942, he helped pull other crew members to safety. When the Navy discovered his age the following year, they gave him a dishonorable discharge. Touted in newspapers as the "baby vet," Graham fought for years to get back his decorations and benefits and to win an honorable discharge retroactively. He eventually succeeded.

Was there a Kilroy?

He was the hero of graffiti scrawled by countless U.S. servicemen during World War II, proclaiming "Kilroy was here," but he may never have existed in person. Sergeant Francis J. Kilroy of the U.S. Air Corps and James J. Kilroy, an inspector in a Massachusetts shipyard, have both been suggested as the namesake of the phrase, but hard evidence is lacking.

How many communists did Senator Joseph McCarthy say he found in the State Department?

In his February 9, 1950, speech in Wheeling, West Virginia, McCarthy brandished a list which he said contained the names of 205 communists, though the number fluctuated over time. For the next few years, McCarthy investigated State Department officials and others, relying on shaky charges and insinuation. He was finally brought down when the Senate voted to censure him in December 1954.

Which of Marilyn Monroe's marriages lasted the longest?
The Hollywood screen goddess (1926–62) was married three times: to aircraft plant worker James Dougherty, baseball hero Joe DiMaggio, and playwright Arthur Miller. The marriage to Miller lasted the longest—nearly five years, from 1956 to 1961. Her marriage as a teenager to Dougherty lasted four years, from 1942 to 1946. The shortest of her marriages was to DiMaggio—nine months in 1954.

How old was John F. Kennedy when Marilyn Monroe sang "Happy Birthday" to him?
He was approaching his 45th birthday when Monroe sang the song to him at a Democratic fund-raiser in Madison Square Garden on March 19, 1962.

How many times was Richard J. Daley mayor of Chicago?
Beginning in 1955, Boss Daley was elected for five terms. He was serving as mayor when he died in 1976. Since 1989, his son, Richard M. Daley, Jr., has served as mayor of Chicago.

What is Wolfman Jack's real name?
Robert Weston Smith. Born in Brooklyn, the disc jockey began broadcasting as the "Wolfman" in 1960 at border station XERF in Via Cuncio, Mexico, just north of Del Rio, Texas. His raunchy, outlaw pronouncements were heard widely in the U.S. but remained beyond the jurisdiction of the FCC.

From what university was Timothy Leary fired?
Harvard. He and fellow professor Richard Alpert were fired for LSD experiments with students.

Who was the voice of the "Crazy Eddie" stereo stores?
A New York disc jockey named Jerry Carroll (also known as Dr. Jerry) did the radio and TV ads for the chain of electronics stores in the Northeast, which began with a store on Kings Highway in Brooklyn in 1972. Although he screamed and yelled at the camera, Carroll himself was not "Crazy Eddie"; that was Eddie Antar, founder of the stores. In 1989 the chain of stores collapsed in scandal, with Antar indicted for defrauding stockholders.

Who was the first native-born American to become a saint in the Roman Catholic Church?
Elizabeth Ann Bayley Seton or "Mother Seton" (1774–1821). Born into a wealthy Episcopalian family in New York City, Seton converted to Roman Catholicism after her husband died. She founded the American Sisters of Charity, an order dedicated to helping the poor and teaching in parish schools. At her canonization ceremony in 1975, Pope Paul VI noted Seton's contributions as wife, mother, widow, and nun. Her feast day is January 4.

How many Hamilton Fishes have there been?
Five, dating back to 1808, when the first Hamilton Fish was born to Nicholas Fish (1758–1833), Revolutionary War patriot and friend of Alexander Hamilton, for whom Nicholas named his son. Each Hamilton Fish was father to another one, in this order:

> Hamilton Fish (1808–93)
> Hamilton Fish (1849–1936)
> Hamilton Fish, Jr. (1888–1991)
> Hamilton Fish, Jr. (1926–)
> Hamilton Fish III (1951–)

The three middle individuals have all served as Republican congressmen from New York. In a break with tradition, Hamilton III is a Democrat who published the left-wing magazine *The Nation* from 1977 to 1987.

Where did Michael Milken go to college?
The insider stock trader who became the symbol of 1980s greed
graduated from the University of California at Berkeley, symbol of
1960s activism, in 1968.

Who are the three richest people in the United States?
According to *Forbes* magazine's 1992 list of richest Americans,
they are:

William Henry Gates 3rd ($6.3 billion)
John Werner Kluge ($5.5 billion)
Helen Walton, S. Robson Walton, Jim C. Walton, John T.
Walton, Alice L. Walton (tied at $5.1 billion each)

Gates is the founder of Microsoft Corporation, the world's largest
personal computer software company. Kluge is an entertainment
tycoon. The Waltons are heirs of Sam Walton, the late founder of
Wal-Mart.

Where does Ross Perot rank on the list?
Forbes puts him at Number 19, with an estimated net worth
of $2.4 billion.

Who coined the nickname "Slick Willie"?
Arkansas newspaper columnist and long-time Clinton opponent
Paul Greenberg was the first to apply the name to then-governor
of Arkansas and future president Bill Clinton.

Popular Culture

How many copies did *Poor Richard's Almanack* sell when it was published?
Over the course of publication (1732–57), Benjamin Franklin's *Almanack* sold on average 10,000 copies per year.

What is the oldest U.S. newspaper still being published?
The *Courant,* published in Hartford, Connecticut, since 1764.

How old is the song "I've Been Working on the Railroad"?
No one knows exactly. It seems to have begun as "The Levee Song" among African-American workers building levees on the Mississippi River in Louisiana in the 1830s–40s. It was later adapted to railroad building and associated with Irish work gangs in the West. By 1880, when almost 100,000 miles of railroad track had been laid, the song was known across the country.

What is "Columbia, the Gem of the Ocean" called in Great Britain?
With lyrics altered to reflect the country, it is called "Britannia, the Pride of the Ocean." Written by Englishmen David T. Shaw and Thomas à Becket, the "Columbia" version (referring to an alternate name for the United States) was first published in 1843

under the name "Columbia, the Land of the Brave"; "Land of the Brave" was later changed to "Gem of the Ocean."

Who was called the "Swedish Nightingale"?
Swedish soprano Jenny Lind, brought to the U.S. by showman P. T. Barnum for a concert tour that lasted from 1850 to 1852. Her highly successful appearances helped to fix opera as a popular art in American culture.

When did the *New York Times* adopt the slogan, "All the news that's fit to print"?
In 1896, when it was purchased by *Chattanooga Times* newspaper publisher Adolph Ochs. Known until 1857 as *The New York Daily Times,* it was founded in 1851 as a Whig newspaper. Under its first editor, Henry Jarvis Raymond, the *Times* was known for its support of Lincoln during the Civil War and its attacks on New York's Boss Tweed. When Adolph Ochs purchased the *Times,* he increased serious news coverage and added a book review and magazine. The paper's weekday edition currently reaches 1.2 million readers; the Sunday edition reaches 1.8 million.

Where was the author of "Swanee River" born?
Stephen Collins Foster, who wrote the song about the South (also called "Old Folks at Home") in 1852, was born near Lawrenceville, Pennsylvania, in 1826.

> *Where was the author of "Dixie" born?*
> Daniel D. Emmett, the author of the 1859 song that became a Confederate anthem, was born in Ohio.

For what U.S. periodical was Karl Marx a correspondent?
In the 1860s, he wrote about politics in Europe for the *New York Tribune.*

How many newspapers did William Randolph Hearst (1863–1951) own?

The man who had been expelled from Harvard bought or started 42 newspapers. Only a handful remained by the time of his death in 1951.

To what war does the song "When Johnny Comes Marching Home" refer?

The song was written in 1863 during the Civil War by Union army bandmaster Patrick S. Gilmore.

Who was Jim Crow?

A black stage character invented by minstrel star Thomas Rice in the decades before the Civil War. The name came to be applied to the segregationist laws that kept blacks separate from whites beginning in the 1870s. The Supreme Court declared Jim Crow laws unconstitutional in *Brown v. Board of Education* in 1954.

Where was the Chautauqua Movement based?

The self-improvement program designed "to promote habits of reading and study in nature, art, science, and in secular and sacred literature, in connection with the routine of daily life" was first proposed at a Methodist Episcopal camp meeting at Lake Chautauqua, New York, in 1873 by Bishop John H. Vincent. In the years that followed, thousands came to the Chautauqua Assembly in New York for eight-week summer programs on the arts, sciences, and religion. From 1912 to about 1924, "traveling Chautauquas" were organized across the country as commercial tent shows featuring lectures and entertainment.

What was Annie Oakley's real name?

The sharpshooter who appeared in Buffalo Bill's Wild West Show in the late 19th century was born Phoebe Mozee. Her life was popularized on Broadway in the 1946 Irving Berlin musical *Annie Get Your Gun,* starring Ethel Merman.

What gave Gibson Girls their name?
The illustrations of fashionable, modern women of the 1890s were named for the artist who drew them for popular magazines—Charles Dana Gibson. Gibson's drawings helped to establish a new standard of American beauty at the turn of the 19th century.

Where was the first public showing of a motion picture in the U.S.?
It took place on April 23, 1896, at New York's Koster & Bial Music Hall on 34th Street and Broadway. The 12 short-subject films, projected on Thomas Edison's Vitascope, accompanied a vaudeville show. Previously, Edison's films could only be viewed peep-show style on his Kinetoscope (invented 1891).

Where was the first nickelodeon?
The forerunner to the modern movie theater first opened in McKeesport, Pennsylvania, near Pittsburgh, in 1905. The nickelodeon showed motion pictures with musical accompaniment.

What was Mr. Dooley's occupation?
The humorous fictional character created by Chicago journalist Finley Peter Dunne was a saloon keeper. He was based on an actual person—Jim McGarry, a Chicago barkeep. He appeared in such satirical works as *Mr. Dooley in Peace and in War* (1898) and *Mr. Dooley in the Hearts of His Countrymen* (1899).

What was the first year of *The Ziegfeld Follies?*
The first in this series of musical shows staged by producer Florenz Ziegfeld was "The Follies of 1907." Combining European style and American topical humor, the show was such a hit that Ziegfeld followed it with 21 annual editions of *The Ziegfeld Follies.* Famous alumni include Will Rogers, Ruth Etting, Eddie Cantor, and W. C. Fields.

What was the first American musical radio broadcast?
It was a broadcast from the Metropolitan Opera House in New York City in 1910.

Which Irving Berlin song came first, "God Bless America" or "White Christmas"?
"God Bless America" (1918) appeared 24 years before "White Christmas" (1942). "God Bless America" was written for, but discarded from, the Broadway musical, *Yip, Yip, Yaphank.* "White Christmas" made its introduction in the 1942 film musical *Holiday Inn,* starring Fred Astaire and Bing Crosby.

> *For what show did Irving Berlin write "Oh, How I Hate to Get Up in the Morning"?*
> Berlin wrote the 1918 song for the show *Yip, Yip, Yaphank,* the same show that generated "God Bless America."

How many songs did Cole Porter (1893–1964) write?
The composer wrote nearly 800 songs and two dozen musicals, including *Kiss Me, Kate* (1948) and *Can-Can* (1953).

What was the first tabloid newspaper?
It was the *Illustrated Daily News* (now the *Daily News*). Founded in New York City in 1919, it was the nation's largest-selling paper by 1925. Current weekday circulation is 781,800; Sunday circulation is 983,000.

With what band did Louis Armstrong make his first recording?
Armstrong's first recordings were with the Creole Jazz Band of Joseph "King" Oliver in Chicago in 1923. Armstrong played second clarinet to Oliver.

When did Josephine Baker first perform in Paris?

Born in St. Louis, Missouri, Baker (1906–75) first danced bare-breasted in *La revue nègre* in Paris in 1925. She later joined the Folies Bergère. She became a French citizen in 1937.

When did Bela Lugosi first play Count Dracula?

The Hungarian actor first played the role onstage in the 1927 Broadway production of *Dracula,* adapted by Hamilton Deane and John Balderston from Bram Stoker's novel. Lugosi became famous by playing Dracula in the 1931 movie version.

What is the source of the Depression-era Democratic party theme song "Happy Days Are Here Again"?

Written by Milton Ager and Jack Yellen, it first appeared in the 1930 MGM musical *Chasing Rainbows,* starring Bessie Love and Charles King. The movie opened after the 1929 stock market crash and was a flop.

Where was the first Academy Awards ceremony held?

In the Blossom Room of the Hollywood Roosevelt Hotel on May 16, 1929. All awards were presented by Douglas Fairbanks, then president of the Academy of Motion Picture Arts and Sciences. There were no surprises because the winners' names had already been made public in February.

Where is it held now?
Since April 14, 1969, it has been held at the Dorothy Chandler Pavilion at the Music Center in Los Angeles.

What were the real first names of the following musicians:
Duke Ellington—Edward
Tommy Dorsey—Francis
Glenn Miller—Alton
Count Basie—William

Where was the first drive-in movie?

It opened on a 40-acre parking lot in Camden, New Jersey, on

June 6, 1933. The creation of New Jersey entrepreneurs Richard M. Hollinshead, Jr., and Willis Smith started a nationwide craze. During its peak, in 1958, there were over 4,000 drive-ins across America. As of 1992, there were fewer than 1,000 drive-ins in operation, none of them in their state of origin.

In what film did Judy Garland sing "Dear Mr. Gable—You Made Me Love You"?

The love song from one MGM star to another appeared in *Broadway Melody of 1938*.

Who wrote the ballad "Rosie the Riveter"?

Jay Loeb and R. Evans were the composers of the popular World War II song. Rosie the Riveter was a nickname for civilian working women during World War II, particularly those who worked in war-related industries.

Who wrote the World War II anthem "Praise the Lord, and Pass the Ammunition"?

It was written by Frank Loesser, the Broadway composer whose musicals include *Guys and Dolls* (1950) and *The Most Happy Fella* (1956).

When did fans of Frank Sinatra riot at the Paramount Theater?

On Columbus Day 1944, at the height of his popularity. Thirty thousand bobbysoxers rioted at the New York theater where Sinatra was performing. It was reported that cries of "Frankie, Frankie!" could be heard blocks away.

What was the first TV sitcom?

The first situation comedy on television was a live show called "Mary Kay and Johnny" (1947–50, Dumont). Forerunner to *I Love Lucy*, the live show concerned the adventurous life of New

York newlyweds Johnny and Mary Kay Stearns. The couple's real-life newborn son was worked into the show in 1948.

When was the LP invented?
A Columbia Records (CBS) team led by Dr. Peter Goldmark invented the long-playing 33⅓ r.p.m. record in 1948 as a successor to the 78 r.p.m. record. To compete with CBS, RCA came up with the handy 45 r.p.m. record in 1949.

On what Damon Runyon story is *Guys and Dolls* based?
The 1950 Broadway musical by Frank Loesser was inspired by the 1933 short story "The Idyll of Miss Sarah Brown," which chronicles the courtship and marriage of gambler Sky Masterson and mission worker Sarah Brown. A revival of *Guys and Dolls* opened on Broadway in spring 1992.

When was the Comics Code Authority introduced?
The comic book industry began to regulate itself with this code in 1954. Among other rules, it required that "Policemen, judges, government officials and respected institutions shall never be presented in such a way as to create disrespect for established authority," and "In every instance good shall triumph over evil and the criminal punished for his misdeeds."

When did Disneyland open? Disney World?
The amusement park opened in Anaheim, California, on July 17, 1955. Its original size was 200 acres. Much bigger than Disneyland, Disney World opened near Orlando, Florida, on October 1, 1971.

What does EPCOT stand for?
The acronym for the third Walt Disney amusement center stands for Experimental Prototype Community of Tomorrow. It opened in 1982 as a Disney World theme park.

Where did "Dear Abby" and "Ann Landers" get their starts?
Abigail Van Buren (born Pauline Esther "Popo" Friedman) and
Ann Landers (born Esther Pauline "Eppie" Friedman) are iden-
tical twins born on July 4, 1918, in Sioux City, Iowa. In 1955,
Eppie took over as Ruth Crowley's replacement on the *Chicago
Sun-Times* "Dear Ann Landers" advice column. In 1956, the other
sister began writing under the tag-line "Dear Abby" at the *San
Francisco Chronicle*.

Did Bob Dylan ever meet Woody Guthrie?
Yes, albeit when Guthrie was in his last years. Born Robert Zim-
merman in 1941 in Duluth, Minnesota, young folksinger Bob
Dylan hitchhiked to New York in 1960 to visit his musical idol
Woody Guthrie, who was hospitalized with Huntington's chorea.
The composer and collector of hundreds of folk songs, Guthrie
(1912–67) inspired a generation of musicians. Dylan's first al-
bum, *Bob Dylan* (1962), included a composition entitled "Song
for Woody."

**Which TV special came first, "Rudolph the Red-Nosed Rein-
deer" or "A Charlie Brown Christmas"?**
"Rudolph" appeared first, in December 1964; "Charlie Brown"
followed in 1965. Since then, both have appeared annually at
Christmastime on CBS.

Where were the following situation comedies set:
  "The Phil Silvers Show" (CBS, 1955–59)—Camp Fremont
    Army Base, Fort Baxter, Roseville, Kansas
  "Leave It To Beaver" (CBS/ABC, 1957–63)—Mayfield, USA
  "The Andy Griffith Show" (CBS, 1960–68)—Mayberry, North
    Carolina
  "The Dick Van Dyke Show" (CBS, 1961–66)—New Rochelle,
    New York
  "Bewitched" (ABC, 1964–72)—Westport, Connecticut

"The Mary Tyler Moore Show" (CBS, 1970–77)—
Minneapolis, Minnesota
"All in the Family" (CBS, 1971–79)—Queens, New York
"Barney Miller" (ABC, 1975–82)—12th Police Precinct,
Greenwich Village, New York
"Cheers" (NBC, 1982–93)—Boston, Massachusetts
"The Cosby Show" (NBC, 1984–92)—Brooklyn, New York
"Roseanne" (ABC, 1988–)—Lanford, Illinois

What town was originally planned as the site of the Woodstock concert?
The Woodstock Music and Art Fair was originally scheduled to take place in Wallkill, New York, but had to be moved to nearby Bethel when Wallkill residents, nervous about the huge turnout, backed out of the deal. The event, held August 15–17, 1969, brought together about 400,000 people. Performers included Jimi Hendrix, Janis Joplin, Joan Baez, Arlo Guthrie, Joe Cocker, Jefferson Airplane, and the Grateful Dead.

What was on the cover of the last issue of *Life* magazine's original run?
The cover of the final issue, December 29, 1972, features "The Year in Pictures 1972" in block letters. *Life* had been in publication for 36 years, beginning November 23, 1936.

Which came first, Betamax or VHS?
Sony introduced the Betamax (or Beta) videocassette recorder in 1975. In 1976, JVC (the Victor Company of Japan) introduced the competing VHS system. By the end of the 1980s, VHS had pushed Beta out of the market, and VCRs had spread across the U.S.

What was Broadway's all-time longest-running show?
A Chorus Line. It ran 6,137 performances from 1975 to 1990. Its

nearest competitor is *Oh! Calcutta!* with 5,959 performances between 1976 and 1989.

Which movie has made more money, *E.T.* or *Star Wars*?
Directed and co-produced by Steven Spielberg, *E.T. The Extraterrestrial* (1982) is the all-time money-making champ at $228.6 million. *Star Wars* (1977), directed by George Lucas, is in second place at $193.5 million. Either individually or together, Spielberg and Lucas have helped create seven of the top ten money-making movies.

For whom are the Nintendo Super Mario Brothers named?
American Nintendo Company employees took the name "Mario" from the landlord of their building. The Nintendo system first appeared in the U.S. in 1986.

How many cable television companies are there in the U.S.?
As of 1990, about 9,000.

What was the "Make-Believe Ballroom"?
It was a long-lived program of American popular music and ballroom music on New York radio station WNEW-AM. Begun in 1934 by announcer Martin Block, it ran until WNEW-AM went off the air on December 11, 1992. It was known for popularizing big band, swing, and jazz, and for its distinctive announcers, such as William B. Williams.

When did Superman die?
The comic book superhero died fighting the villain Doomsday in *Superman* No. 75, the January 1993 issue that went on sale on November 11, 1992.

Presidents

Who were the members of President George Washington's first cabinet?
At the outset of his first term (1789–93), they were:

Thomas Jefferson—Secretary of State
Alexander Hamilton—Secretary of the Treasury
Henry Knox—Secretary of War
Edmund Randolph—Attorney General

What president was known as "His Rotundity"?
John Adams (served 1797–1801).

What was the Virginia dynasty?
They were four of the first five presidents, all from Virginia:

George Washington (served 1789–97)
Thomas Jefferson (served 1801–09)
James Madison (served 1809–17)
James Monroe (served 1817–25)

John Adams of Massachusetts (served 1797–1801) was the only one of the first five presidents not from Virginia. His son John

Quincy Adams broke the hold of the Virginia dynasty by taking office as president 1825–29.

What was the name of the slave reputed to have been Thomas Jefferson's mistress?

Sally Hemings. The charge that he had fathered children by her while he was an envoy in Paris came up during the presidential election of 1804, which he won just the same.

What president was nicknamed "Old Hickory"?

Andrew Jackson, president from 1829 to 1837. He received the nickname during the War of 1812 because of his tough physical and personal character.

Why was he called the "farmer from Tennessee"?

Because he made his home there and had helped frame its state constitution. However, his birthplace was not in Tennessee but in Waxhaw on the border between North and South Carolina.

Who belonged to Andrew Jackson's "Kitchen Cabinet"?

The unofficial group of advisors to the president, active mainly during his first term (1829–1833), included:

Amos Kennedy, newspaper editor from Kentucky
Andrew J. Donelson, Jackson's personal secretary
William B. Lewis, an old military comrade
Martin Van Buren, secretary of state
John H. Eaton, secretary of war
Duff Green, newspaper editor; replaced in midterm by Francis
    J. Blair

What president gave the longest recorded inauguration speech?

On March 4, 1841, William Henry Harrison gave the longest address, at about 8,500 words. Harrison delivered the 100-minute speech outdoors without an overcoat in bitterly cold weather. He caught pneumonia and died on April 4, 1841, one month after taking office.

What president gave the shortest inaugural address?
At his second inaugural in March 1793, George Washington gave the shortest address—135 words.

What president was known as "His Accidency"?
John Tyler, because he moved up from the vice-presidency through the accident of President William Henry Harrison's death from pneumonia in 1841.

Who was the first President whom Congress tried to impeach?
In 1843, a Congressional committee put forth a resolution of impeachment against President John Tyler, for abusing the power of the veto. The resolution was defeated 127 to 83, and Tyler was not impeached.

Who was the first president to have a veto overridden by Congress?
John Tyler in 1845.

How many presidents have served as speaker of the House of Representatives?
Only one—James K. Polk (president 1845–49). He was speaker of the House from 1835 to 1839.

Who was the last Whig president?
Millard Fillmore (1850–53) was the last president from the Whig party. Three other presidents were Whigs: William Henry Harri-

son (1841), John Tyler (1841–45), and Zachary Taylor (1849–50).

How many presidents never married?
Only one—James Buchanan (president 1857–61).

Where was Abraham Lincoln born?
The 16th president was born in Hardin County (now Larue County), Kentucky on February 12, 1809. He eventually settled in Springfield, Illinois. He was assassinated on April 15, 1865.

How old was Abraham Lincoln when he was first elected to public office?
Lincoln was 25 when he was elected to the Illinois state legislature as an assemblyman in 1834.

How many presidents have registered patents?
Just one—Abraham Lincoln. He secured patent 6469 for a plan to buoy steamboats over shoals.

By what percentage did Abraham Lincoln win the Presidency?
In a contest with four candidates in 1860 (Lincoln, Stephen Douglas, John C. Bell, and John C. Breckinridge), Lincoln received 40 percent of the popular vote and carried 18 states.

Who were Lincoln's vice-presidents?
During his first term (1861–65), it was Hannibal Hamlin of Maine. During his second term (1865), it was Andrew Johnson of North Carolina, who succeeded Lincoln upon his assassination.

Did any U.S. president serve in the Confederate government?
One did. John Tyler (president 1841–45) represented Virginia in the Confederate House of Representatives beginning in 1861.

Have any presidents served nonconsecutive terms?
Only one. Grover Cleveland was president from 1885 to 1889.

After being defeated by Republican Benjamin Harrison in the 1888 election, the Democrat Cleveland defeated Harrison in 1892 and won a nonconsecutive second term (1893–97).

Who was the first president to hold a press conference?
Woodrow Wilson, in 1913.

Who was the first president to ride in an automobile to his inauguration?
Warren G. Harding, on March 4, 1921.

Who was the first president to speak over the radio?
Warren G. Harding, on June 14, 1922.

To which president's death was the question asked, "How can they tell?"
Humorist Dorothy Parker made the quip after President Calvin Coolidge's death in 1933.

What president put down the Boston police strike?
Calvin Coolidge, then governor of Massachusetts, called out the state militia to break the strike by Boston police officers in 1919. The praise Coolidge received helped get him elected as Warren G. Harding's vice-president in 1920. Coolidge served as president from 1923 to 1929.

Which was larger—the landslide that elected Herbert Hoover to the presidency in 1928 or the landslide that removed him in 1932?
By the electoral votes of two states, the 1932 landslide was more complete. In 1928, Hoover captured the electoral votes of 40 states; in 1932 Franklin D. Roosevelt captured the votes of 42 states. Roosevelt's landslide was larger in the popular vote as well. The 1928 election saw Hoover winning 6.4 million votes more

than his opponent Alfred E. Smith, while in 1932, Roosevelt won 7 million more votes than Hoover.

When did Roosevelt first use the term "New Deal" to describe his program for recovery?
He first used it in his acceptance speech for the presidential nomination at the 1932 Democratic National Convention in Chicago.

What was Franklin Roosevelt's rank during World War I?
During that war (1917–18) he was the assistant secretary of the Navy.

What were the starting and ending points of Franklin Roosevelt's Hundred Days?
The period, which represented the first session of the first New Deal Congress, lasted from March 9 to June 16, 1933. It was a time of intense legislative activity aimed at reversing the effects of the Depression.

For how many of those Hundred Days did Franklin Roosevelt order the U.S. banks closed?
He ordered them closed March 6–9, 1933.

What relation were Franklin Roosevelt and Winston Churchill?
They were seventh cousins, once removed.

Who was the first president to make a televised speech from the White House?
Harry Truman.

Where did Harry Truman attend college?
He didn't. He was the only president in the 20th century without a college education.

When did the Democrats consider Dwight D. Eisenhower for the presidential nomination?
In 1948, some Democratic leaders looked for a more popular candidate than the controversial Harry Truman. Before eventually nominating Truman, they approached Supreme Court Justice William O. Douglas and former Supreme Allied Commander Eisenhower.

What kind of dog was Checkers?
The canine that gave the title to the 1952 speech by vice-presidential candidate Richard M. Nixon was a cocker spaniel. In the speech, Nixon defended his financial integrity and refused to return the pet given to his children by a supporter.

Who was the first president born in the 20th century?
John F. Kennedy, on May 29, 1917.

By what percentage of the popular vote did John F. Kennedy beat Richard Nixon in 1960?
Although he received 303 electoral votes to Nixon's 219, the popular vote was very close. Kennedy won by 118,550 votes, which represented 2/10 of 1 percent of the popular vote.

What was Sargent Shriver's relation to John F. Kennedy?
Shriver, director of the Peace Corps during Kennedy's term (1961–63), was Kennedy's brother-in-law.

What is Lady Bird Johnson's real name?
President Lyndon Johnson's first lady was born Claudia Alta Taylor.

How many people were on President Richard Nixon's enemies list?
Twenty people were named in the 1971 memo released to the Senate Watergate Committee in 1973. There were 200 additional

enemies on a separate list. The memo proposed the use of "federal machinery," including IRS audits and litigation, to "screw our political enemies." The top 20 enemies included Ed Guthman, national editor of the *Los Angeles Times;* Ronald Dellums, California congressman; Daniel Schorr, CBS reporter; and Paul Newman, actor involved in "radic-lib causes."

Who was the first president to visit the Soviet capital of Moscow while in office?
Richard Nixon in 1972.

With how many counts of impeachment was Richard Nixon charged?
Three. On July 30, 1974, the House Judiciary Committee charged the president with three counts related to the Watergate case: obstructing justice; abuse of power; and defying the House Judiciary Committee subpoenas.

When did Spiro Agnew resign from the vice-presidency?
October 10, 1973.

When did Richard Nixon resign from the presidency?
Less than a year later, on August 9, 1974, at 11:35 A.M.

Who replaced them?
Gerald R. Ford replaced both. As representative from Michigan and House minority leader, Ford was chosen to replace Agnew as vice-president, then succeeded to the presidency on Nixon's resignation.

Who was the first president to have more than one woman in his cabinet?
Jimmy Carter (served 1977–81). His female cabinet members were:

Patricia Roberts Harris—Housing and Urban Development;
    later moved to Health and Human Services
Shirley Mount Hufstedler—Education
Juanita Kreps—Commerce

While in office, where did President Jimmy Carter teach Sunday school?
At First Baptist Church in Washington, D.C.

What was Ronald Reagan's first broadcasting job?
In his first job after college, the future president (served 1981–89) broadcasted play-by-play accounts of major league baseball games from Station WHO in Des Moines, Iowa.

When did Ronald Reagan appear as host of "General Electric Theater"?
Reagan served as host and commercial spokesman on the CBS dramatic anthology from 1954 to 1962. The show aired Sundays from 9:00–9:30 P.M. Reagan occasionally starred in the dramas showcased in the series, including "Money and the Minister," where he acted opposite his wife, Nancy Davis.

Who is Maureen Reagan's mother?
Jane Wyman, Ronald Reagan's first wife (married 1940, divorced 1948). Nancy Davis Reagan (married 1952) is her stepmother.

When did Ronald Reagan joke about bombing the Soviet Union?
Reagan made the joke a few minutes before his weekly radio broadcast on August 11, 1984. He said, "My fellow Americans, I am pleased to announce I just signed legislation that will outlaw Russia forever. We begin bombing in five minutes."

Which president said, "Fluency in English is something that I'm not often accused of"?

George Bush, in a toast to Pakistani Prime Minister Benazir Bhutto at a White House dinner on June 6, 1989.

Where did President Bush do his Christmas shopping when he was trying to set an example of consumer confidence?
On November 29, 1991, in the midst of a recession, Bush went shopping at the Frederick Towne Mall in Frederick, Maryland. Among his purchases were a pair of socks at J.C. Penney's.

What was Bill Clinton's name at birth?
The 42nd president (1993–) was born William Jefferson Blythe 4th on August 19, 1946. His father, a traveling salesman, died in a car accident three months before he was born. He received his new name when his mother married Roger Clinton, a car dealer, in 1950.

Where did Bill Clinton grow up?
He was born in the small town of Hope, Arkansas, but was raised in the city of Hot Springs from the age of four.

Who was the tallest president?
Abraham Lincoln (1861–1865) at six feet, four inches.

   Who was the shortest?
   James Madison (1809–1817) at five feet, four inches.

Who was the heaviest president?
William Howard Taft, at a top weight of 352 pounds.

How many presidents attended Harvard University?
Five:

   John Adams
   John Quincy Adams
   Theodore Roosevelt

Franklin D. Roosevelt
John F. Kennedy

Who was the first president to write an autobiography?
The tradition began with the nation's second president, John
Adams.

Who was the youngest man to become president of the U.S.?
Theodore Roosevelt, who was a 42 year-old vice president when
he took office upon the assassination of President William Mc-
Kinley in 1901. At 43, John F. Kennedy was the youngest man to
be elected president.

Who was the oldest man to be elected president?
Ronald Reagan, at 69 in 1980 and at 73 in 1984.

**How many presidents are buried in Arlington National Cem-
etery?**
Two: William Howard Taft and John Fitzgerald Kennedy.

The Question and Answer Hall of Fame

Which presidents are carved on Mount Rushmore?
From left to right, they are George Washington, Thomas Jefferson, Abraham Lincoln, and Theodore Roosevelt.

When did Benjamin Franklin fly his kite in a thunderstorm?
Franklin performed the experiment that proved lightning is electricity in 1751.

How many federal holidays are there?
There are 10 federal legal public holidays:

New Year's Day
Martin Luther King Day
Washington's Birthday (a.k.a. Presidents' Day)
Memorial Day
Independence Day
Labor Day
Columbus Day
Veterans' Day
Thanksgiving
Christmas

Whose faces are on the following denominations of U.S. paper currency?

One dollar—George Washington
Two dollars—Thomas Jefferson
Five dollars—Abraham Lincoln
Ten dollars—Alexander Hamilton
Twenty dollars—Andrew Jackson
Fifty dollars—Ulysses S. Grant
One hundred dollars—Benjamin Franklin

How many people signed the Mayflower Compact?
Forty-one, in 1620.

How many signed the Declaration of Independence?
Fifty-six delegates plus Secretary Charles Thomson, beginning in 1776.

How many signed the U.S. Constitution?
Thirty-nine delegates plus Secretary William Jackson, in 1787.

What did the battle cry "fifty-four forty or fight" mean?
This was the slogan of U.S. expansionists who wanted to fix the boundary of the Oregon country (the Pacific Northwest) at latitude 54° 40' N., in the middle of what is now British Columbia in Canada. The belligerent slogan was associated with the presidential campaign of James K. Polk in 1844. Despite the bluster, Polk's administration agreed to fix the boundary at 49° N. in 1846.

Who was "Old Rough and Ready"?
General Zachary Taylor, hero of the Mexican War (1846–48) and president from 1849 to 1850. Taylor got the nickname for his plain habits and blunt demeanor.

Who was "Old Fuss and Feathers"?
General Winfield Scott, who also led troops in the Mexican War. Scott's vain and blustering ways earned him his nickname.

What states were in the Union during the Civil War? What states were in the Confederacy?

Twenty-five states were in the Union by the end of the Civil War; 11 were in the Confederacy. The states were:

Union	Confederacy
California	Alabama
Connecticut	Arkansas
Delaware	Florida
Illinois	Georgia
Indiana	Louisiana
Iowa	Mississippi
Kansas	North Carolina
Kentucky	South Carolina
Maine	Tennessee
Maryland	Texas
Massachusetts	Virginia
Michigan	
Minnesota	
Missouri	
Nevada	
New Hampshire	
New Jersey	
New York	
Ohio	
Oregon	
Pennsylvania	
Rhode Island	
Vermont	
West Virginia	
Wisconsin	

In what year was each state admitted to the Union?
The 50 states, with their dates of admission, are listed below. The original 13 states are marked with an asterisk.

Alabama—1819	Montana—1889
Alaska—1959	Nebraska—1867
Arizona—1912	Nevada—1864
Arkansas—1836	New Hampshire—1788*
California—1850	New Jersey—1787*
Colorado—1876	New Mexico—1912
Connecticut—1788*	New York—1788*
Delaware—1787*	North Carolina—1789*
Florida—1845	North Dakota—1889
Georgia—1788*	Ohio—1803
Hawaii—1959	Oklahoma—1907
Idaho—1890	Oregon—1859
Illinois—1818	Pennsylvania—1787*
Indiana—1816	Rhode Island—1790*
Iowa—1846	South Carolina—1788*
Kansas—1861	South Dakota—1889
Kentucky—1792	Tennessee—1796
Louisiana—1812	Texas—1845
Maine—1820	Utah—1896
Maryland—1788*	Vermont—1791
Massachusetts—1788*	Virginia—1788*
Michigan—1837	Washington—1889
Minnesota—1858	West Virginia—1863
Mississippi—1817	Wisconsin—1848
Missouri—1821	Wyoming—1890

How long is the Gettysburg Address?
The speech, given by Abraham Lincoln on November 19, 1863, runs 271 words, if you count "resting place" as two words.

Who said, "I will fight no more forever"?
The pledge was uttered by Nez Percé chief Joseph (c. 1840–

1904) in 1877. It was part of a larger statement made when his fugitive tribe surrendered to the U.S. Army following a long, grueling journey as they attempted to flee to Canada. The exact quote is, "Hear me, my chiefs, I am tired; my heart is sick and sad. From where the sun now stands, I will fight no more forever."

What is the score at the end of the game in "Casey at the Bat"?

Two to four, with the "Mudville nine" losing to an anonymous team thanks to "Mighty Casey" striking out in the ninth inning. Written by Ernest Lawrence Thayer (1863–1940), the poem was first published pseudonymously in the *San Francisco Examiner* on June 3, 1888.

Who is buried in Grant's Tomb?

Ulysses S. Grant and his wife Julia Denton Grant are buried in the tomb on Manhattan's Upper West Side.

Which presidential candidate offered a "square deal"?

Theodore Roosevelt.

Which offered a "new deal"?
Franklin Delano Roosevelt.

Which offered a "fair deal"?
Harry Truman.

How many episodes of the TV series "I Love Lucy" were broadcast?

One hundred seventy-nine, from 1951 to 1957, on CBS.

How many episodes of the TV series "The Honeymooners" were broadcast?
Thirty-nine, from 1955 to 1956, also on CBS.

What is the first election district to vote and report its returns in presidential elections?
Dixville Notch, New Hampshire.

Does the song "Louie Louie" contain dirty lyrics?
Generations of fans and enemies of rock and roll have thought that it does, but in all probability it does not. The original song as written and recorded by Richard Berry in 1956 has tame lyrics about longing to see a certain girl while sailing across the Caribbean Sea. However, in the hit version by the Kingsmen of Portland, Oregon, in 1963, the lyrics are so blurred that listeners can make it mean anything they want. Rumors of obscene lyrics sparked an official investigation in 1963, but the FCC reported that it "found the record to be unintelligible."

Quotations

Who first said "Taxation without representation is tyranny"?
No one knows for sure. Lawyer James Otis is often credited with
having coined the phrase in 1761, but the evidence for that is
shaky. The exact words did not appear in print until 1820, when
John Adams recalled them in some notes.

Who coined the phrase "the shot heard round the world"?
American poet and philosopher Ralph Waldo Emerson originated
the phrase in his poem "Concord Hymn" (1836). The poem
memorialized the Battle of Lexington and Concord of 1775, the
first battle of the War of Independence.

**Did Priscilla Mullins ever say to John Alden, "Why don't you
speak for yourself, John?"**
The line is a fabrication of Henry Wadsworth Longfellow, found
in his poem "The Courtship of Miles Standish" (1858). Alden,
Mullins, and Standish were all passengers on the Mayflower but
were not known to be involved in a love triangle.

**Who said, "He that lies down with dogs, shall rise up with
fleas"?**

Benjamin Franklin in *Poor Richard's Almanack* (published 1732–57).

Who called George Washington "first in war, first in peace, and first in the hearts of his countrymen"?
Henry Lee, a fellow officer in the Revolutionary War and the father of Civil War general Robert E. Lee.

Who said, "A little rebellion now and then is a good thing"?
Thomas Jefferson, writing from Paris on hearing of Shays's Rebellion, an uprising of poor farmers against the Massachusetts state government in 1786. Jefferson added, "God forbid that we should ever be twenty years without such a rebellion."

Who said, "I am not among those who fear the people; they, and not the rich, are our dependence for continued freedom"?
Thomas Jefferson.

Who said, "I have not yet begun to fight"?
Scottish-born American privateer John Paul Jones in 1779, during the Revolutionary War.

Who said, "We have met the enemy, and they are ours"?
Oliver Hazard Perry at the Battle of Lake Erie in 1813, during the War of 1812.

Who said, "Our country, right or wrong"?
Naval officer Stephen Decatur, hero of campaigns against Barbary Coast privateers and the War of 1812. Decatur made his famous remark in a toast at a dinner in Norfolk, Virginia, in 1815: "Our country! In her intercourse with foreign nations may she always be in the right. But our country, right or wrong."

Who said, "I would rather be right than be president"?
Statesman Henry Clay (1777–1852).

Who said, "After eight years as president, I have only two regrets: that I have not shot Henry Clay or hanged John C. Calhoun"?
Andrew Jackson.

In what election did a politician profess to regret "the necessity, real or imaginary, which has been supposed to exist, of appealing to the feelings and passions of our countrymen, rather than to their reasons and their judgments"?
The remark was made by Henry Clay, leader of the Whig party, after its candidate William Henry Harrison won the 1840 presidential election with a campaign marked by simplistic images and untruths.

Who said of Americans, "If I were asked . . . to what the singular prosperity and growing strength of that people ought mainly to be attributed, I should reply: To the superiority of their women"?
Alexis de Tocqueville, author of *Democracy in America* (1835, 1840).

Who said, "A foolish consistency is the hobgoblin of little minds"?
Ralph Waldo Emerson, in the essay "Self-Reliance" (1841). The complete quote is, "A foolish consistency is the hobgoblin of little minds, adored by little statesmen and philosophers and divines."

When did the term "manifest destiny" first appear?
It appeared in an article by John L. O'Sullivan in the July–August 1845 *United States Magazine and Democratic Review*. In the article, O'Sullivan said it was "our manifest destiny to overspread the continent allotted by Providence for the free development of our yearly multiplying millions."

Of whom did Harry Truman say, "He can lie out of both sides of his mouth at the same time, and if he ever caught himself telling the truth, he'd lie just to keep his hand in"?
Truman said it of Richard Nixon.

When did Lincoln say, "I believe this government can not endure permanently half slave and half free"?
In a speech delivered on June 16, 1858, in Springfield, Illinois, accepting the Republican nomination for the U.S. Senate. In the same speech, Lincoln paraphrased the New Testament, saying, "A house divided against itself can not stand."

Who said, "If nominated I will not run. If elected I will not serve"?
Union General William Tecumseh Sherman, when the Republicans tried to draft him for president upon his retirement from the army in 1880.

Who said, "Man is the only animal that blushes. Or needs to"?
Mark Twain.

Who said, "All I have I owe to advertising"?
It was late 19th-century cold cereal developer C. W. Post, whose creations included Grape-Nuts.

To whom is William Randolph Hearst alleged to have said, "You furnish the pictures and I'll furnish the war"?
To artist Frederic Remington, who was covering conditions in Cuba at a time when newspaper publisher Hearst was interested in fomenting war with Spain, then in charge of Cuba. The Spanish-American War of 1898 resulted in part from the trumpeting of Spanish atrocities in newspapers controlled by Hearst and his rivals.

Who said, "Now look! That damned cowboy is president of the United States"?
Senator Mark Hanna of Ohio said it of Theodore Roosevelt in 1901.

Who said, "What this country needs is a really good five-cent cigar"?
It was uttered by Thomas R. Marshall, vice-president under Woodrow Wilson (1913–21), in response to a senator's long speech about the country's needs.

Who said, "Puritanism is the haunting fear that someone, somewhere, may be happy"?
H. L. Mencken.

Who said, "There are no second acts in American lives"?
F. Scott Fitzgerald.

Who said, "The business of America is business"?
President Calvin Coolidge, in a 1925 speech.

In which election year did Calvin Coolidge make his famous announcement declining to run for president?
Coolidge's announcement was: "I do not choose to run for president in 1928."

Who said, "We don't know what we want, but we are ready to bite somebody to get it"?
Will Rogers.

Who called television a "vast wasteland"?
In a 1961 speech, Newton Minow, the chairman of the Federal Communications Commission, announced that television was a "vast wasteland" because it was a "procession" of formulaic and violent programs and endless commercials.

On what occasion did President Eisenhower warn against the "military-industrial complex"?
In his farewell address of January 17, 1961, a few days before Kennedy took office, Eisenhower said: "In the councils of government, we must guard against the acquisition of unwarranted influence, whether sought or unsought, by the military-industrial complex."

About what town did an Army official say, "It became necessary to destroy the town to save it"?
The quote refers to the bombardment of the city of Ben Tre, South Vietnam, during the Tet Offensive in 1968. The army major who said it was unidentified.

Who created the phrase "a thousand points of light"?
Peggy Noonan, in a speech she wrote for presidential nominee George Bush at the 1988 Republican Convention.

What was Vice-President Dan Quayle's version of the United Negro College Fund slogan, "A mind is a terrible thing to waste"?
"What a waste it is to lose one's mind, or not to have a mind is being very wasteful. How true that is." Quayle was speaking at an NAACP luncheon in Nashville, Tennessee, on May 15, 1989.

To whom did George Bush say, "Don't cry for me, Argentina"?
Not to Argentina, but to employees of the Liberty Mutual Insurance Company in Dover, New Hampshire, on January 15, 1992. He was asking people not to feel sorry for him during his tough campaign against Pat Buchanan in the New Hampshire presidential primary.

Reformers and Radicals

Which of the 13 Colonies was founded by pacifists?
Pennsylvania, founded by William Penn, a Quaker, in 1682.
Members of the Society of Friends, or Quaker movement, rejected
formal sacraments and clergy, trusted in the inspiration of an
"inner light," and forbade violence and war. Penn hoped Pennsylvania's government would embody Quaker principles, practic-
ing pacifism and showing justice and charity to Native Americans
and the poor. These hopes were not always realized, but colonial
Quakers tried their best—for example, helping to negotiate a
peace with the Delaware and Shawnee nations during the French
and Indian War.

Where did the Shakers get their name?
Formally known as the "United Society of Believers in Christ's
Second Appearing," this sect got its name from the involuntary
trembling of its members during moments of religious ecstasy.
Founded in England by Mother Ann Lee, the Shakers came to
America in 1774. Lee's followers practiced celibacy, communal
ownership, and sacred dancing. By the 1820s, there were more
than a dozen communities, with 4,000 members. Few Shakers
remain today.

Why was Henry David Thoreau sentenced to jail?
In 1846, the 29-year-old Thoreau was charged with nonpayment

of a poll tax. Thoreau refused to pay because the tax was to be spent on the Mexican War, which he opposed. Thoreau's friends paid the tax for him, after he spent the night of July 23, 1846, in jail. He described the experience in his 1849 essay, "Civil Disobedience."

Where is Harpers Ferry, site of John Brown's abolitionist raid?

It is in what is now West Virginia (then part of Virginia). John Brown led a party of 22 in seizing the U.S. arsenal there in October 1859. Brown, an abolitionist born in Torrington, Connecticut, planned to arm the local slaves and start a full-scale rebellion, but his plan was foiled by state and federal troops. Convicted of treason and murder, Brown was hanged on December 2, 1859.

Who was the first presidential nominee of the Populist Party?

The People's (or Populist) Party nominated James Baird Weaver, a Union general from Iowa, as their presidential candidate at their first national convention on July 4, 1892. His running mate was James C. Field, a Confederate general from Virginia. The party was supported by farmers and workers discontented with the dominant parties.

What was the Wisconsin Idea?

It was a plan for reform created by Wisconsin Governor Robert M. La Follette in the early 1900s. This first statewide progressive reform plan was designed to erode the corruption of political bosses and big business, particularly the railroad trust.

From what literary work is the term "muckraker" derived?

President Teddy Roosevelt drew this unflattering nickname for early 20th-century investigative reporters from the 17th-century allegory *Pilgrim's Progress* by John Bunyan. In this book, a muckraker is a worker too busy gathering dirt and debris to see the celestial crown overhead.

When was the Socialist Party of America founded?
It was born in 1901 under the leadership of Eugene V. Debs. Instead of emphasizing state control of the economy, it advocated worker-protection laws, many of which later came to be enacted. Among the party's goals were the reduction of hours in the workday, nationalization of railroads, and the creation of unemployment insurance.

Who said, "I aimed for the heart and by accident I hit the stomach instead"?
Upton Sinclair. He was discussing the national response to his 1906 novel *The Jungle* about the Chicago meatpacking industry. The book was meant to galvanize workers to socialism but instead led to the passage of the first nationwide food and drug control laws.

In what period did the American Communist party reach its peak membership?
The American Communist party was never so popular as during World War II, when the United States and the Soviet Union were allies. Founded soon after the Bolshevik Revolution of 1917, the party reached a peak membership of about 100,000 during World War II. Afterward, Cold War repression made it unsafe to stay in the party and membership fell.

How long has *The Catholic Worker* been in publication?
The Catholic anarchist and pacifist newspaper founded by Dorothy Day and Peter Maurin has been published since May 1933. The cost, then and now, is one cent per copy.

Who was chairman of the America First Committee?
The chairman of the committee formed in 1940 to oppose U.S.

intervention in World War II was Robert E. Wood, head of Sears, Roebuck. America First's most famous spokesman, however, was aviator Charles A. Lindbergh. Some committee members expressed sympathy for Nazi ideology; Lindbergh had visited Nazi Germany and accepted a medal from Hermann Goering in 1938. Other America Firsters argued more narrowly that neutrality was safer for the U.S. than military intervention.

What is the other America in *The Other America*?
The title of the 1962 book by Michael Harrington refers to the huge number of Americans at the time who were living below the poverty level. According to Harrington, the poor totaled 20–25 percent of the U.S. population, or about 40–50 million people.

What did SDS stand for?
Students for a Democratic Society. The "New Left" movement for social and political change was organized at Port Huron, Michigan, in June 1962. Its manifesto was called the "Port Huron Statement."

When was English first introduced into the Roman Catholic mass in the U.S.?
Partial use of English was introduced to the U.S. liturgy on November 29, 1964. Latin was not completely phased out of the liturgy until Easter 1970.

What car's safety defects did Ralph Nader expose in *Unsafe at Any Speed*?
The Chevrolet Corvair, made by General Motors. Nader's crusading book, published in 1965, led to passage of the Traffic and Motor Vehicle Safety Act of 1966.

Where was the "World's First Human Be-In"?
The counter-cultural gathering for 20,000 hippies and flower children was held in Golden Gate Park, San Francisco, in January

1967. Timothy Leary and poet Allen Ginsberg were among the speakers.

Where was the draft office where the Berrigan brothers burned draft files in 1968?

Catonsville, Maryland. Philip and Daniel Berrigan, both priests, broke into the draft office with seven other Roman Catholic protestors and burned over 600 draft files with napalm. The Berrigans were arrested and convicted, but Daniel jumped bail and went underground for several months before being recaptured.

Was it the "Chicago Seven" or the "Chicago Eight" who were tried for inciting a riot at the 1968 Democratic National Convention?

They began as the "Eight" but were reduced to the "Seven" when defendant Bobby Seale's case was declared a mistrial. Tried in 1969–70 for crossing state lines to riot and conspiring to use interstate commerce to induce rioting at the 1968 Democratic convention in Chicago, the remaining seven were:

Rennie Davis
David Dellinger
John Froines
Tom Hayden
Abbie Hoffman
Jerry Rubin
Lee Weiner

Froines and Weiner were found not guilty of either charge. The other five defendants were convicted of crossing state lines to riot, but their convictions were overturned on appeal. Most of the contempt-of-court findings against the defendants—made in response to their defiant and satiric behavior in the courtroom—were also overturned.

How many students were shot during the antiwar demonstration at Kent State University on May 4, 1970?
Thirteen students were shot by Ohio National Guard troops under the command of General Robert H. Canterbury. Nine were wounded and four were killed: Allison Krause, Jeffrey Miller, Sandra Scheuer, and Bill Schroeder. Of those four, only Krause and Miller had been demonstrating. Scheuer and Schroeder were bystanders.

When did the Pentagon Papers first appear in the *New York Times*?
This classified history of American involvement in Vietnam first began to run in the *New York Times* on June 13, 1971. Despite legal challenges from the White House, the Supreme Court permitted the *Times* and the *Washington Post* to continue publishing the documents. Leaked by former Pentagon employee Daniel Ellsberg, the papers detailed three decades of federal deception and incompetence regarding Vietnam.

What office did Harvey Milk hold?
Harvey Milk (1930–78) was the first openly homosexual candidate to be elected to San Francisco's Board of Supervisors. An advocate of gay rights and urban issues, Milk was elected in 1977, representing the Castro district. He was assassinated, with Mayor George Moscone, by a former supervisor on November 27, 1978.

How many couples were married in the first mass wedding performed by the Rev. Sun Myung Moon?
The head of the Unification Church married 2,075 couples in a mass wedding at Madison Square Garden in New York City on July 1, 1982.

How many Americans did Jonathan Kozol estimate were illiterate in his book *Illiterate America* (1985)?
Kozol said that as of 1984, 25 million Americans were function-

ally illiterate (reading not at all or at less than fifth grade level) and an additional 35 million were marginally illiterate (reading at less than ninth grade level). The total of 60 million represented more than a third of the adult population.

When did Jerry Falwell disband the Moral Majority?
Falwell disbanded the conservative Christian movement in 1989, ten years after founding it. After fighting for such positions as prayer in public schools and a ban on abortions, the organization ended about the same time as Ronald Reagan's presidency, which its influence had helped bring about.

How many card-carrying members of the ACLU are there?
.Founded in 1920, the American Civil Liberties Union, a nonpartisan organization devoted to protecting constitutional rights, has nearly 300,000 members. George Bush used the term "card-carrying member of the ACLU" to darken the name of his opponent Michael Dukakis in the 1988 presidential campaign.

Regional History

Where is Okefenokee Swamp?
The freshwater and cypress swamp, best known as the locale of Walt Kelly's comic strip "Pogo," begins near Waycross, Georgia, and extends into Florida. Its name is a variation of the Indian term "Owaquaphenoga," or "trembling earth."

Where is "Old Smoky"?
The subject of the 1840s folk song "On Top of Old Smoky" is one of the peaks in the Blue Ridge Mountains, located near Asheville, North Carolina.

Where did Peoria, Illinois, get its name?
From the Peoria tribe of the Illinois Confederacy. The name means "carrying a pack on his back."

For how long was the state of California an independent country?
After a revolt on July 4, 1846, led by John C. Frémont against Mexico during the Mexican War, California was declared an independent country for a few days. During its brief independence, California flew the flag of a bear. The California grizzly bear is now the state animal.

Where is the Red River valley?
The Red River begins in New Mexico, serves as the boundary between Texas and Oklahoma, and flows into Louisiana. "The Red River Valley" is the site of the departing lover in the traditional Southern folk song of that name.

How large is Deadwood, South Dakota?
The famous mining town from the gold rush days that now stands as the final resting place for Wild Bill Hickok and Calamity Jane, has 1,830 inhabitants. Every August it relives its frontier past in a three-day "Days of '76" celebration, featuring a historical parade and rodeos. In 1992, Deadwood held its 70th "Days of '76" celebration.

What are the tallest hills in San Francisco?
The tallest are Twin Peaks, Mount Davidson, and Mount Sutro, all more than 900 feet tall. The best known hills—Nob Hill and Telegraph Hill—are smaller, between 300 and 400 feet.

Where did Wall Street get its name?
From the wall built around Lower Manhattan in colonial times to protect cattle from Indian raids.

What is the "Thunderer of Waters"?
It is the Indian name for Niagara Falls, New York.

What does "Detroit" mean?
It is French for "the strait." It refers to the strait formed by the Detroit River between Lake Erie and Lake St. Clair. Originally founded as a French fort and trading post in 1701, Detroit was incorporated as a city in 1815.

Where was the first beaver-hat factory in America?
Founded in 1780 by Zadoc Benedict, it was located in Danbury,

Connecticut. As late as the early 20th century, two thirds of the mills in this town were engaged in hat making.

Who was Cleveland named for?
The city of Cleveland (pop. 573,822) was named for its founder Moses Cleaveland in 1836. The city was once known as the "Forest City" because of its abundance of trees.

Who was the "Hoosier" behind the term "hoosier"?
The source of the term for Indiana residents is often said to be Samuel Hoosier, a contractor for the Ohio Falls Canal in Louisville, Ohio, in 1825. Hoosier's employees, recruited from Indiana, were known as the "Hoosier men" or simply "Hoosiers." By 1833, the term was being used in local periodicals—for example, in a poem in the *Indianapolis Journal* called "The Hoosier Nest."

Who is Dubuque named for?
The city in Iowa is named for French-Canadian Julien Dubuque, who first settled the region in 1785. The town received the name at its founding in 1833.

Where was the Comstock Lode first discovered?
The gold and silver ore deposit was discovered in 1859 in what is now Virginia City, Nevada.

What artwork is housed in the Cyclorama Building in Atlanta?
The 1921 site houses the Cyclorama of the Battle of Atlanta, a depiction of the Civil War battle for control of the Georgia railroad on July 22, 1864. The 1885–86 artwork blends an enormous circular painting with a three-dimensional model of the action. The painting is 358 feet in circumference and 42 feet tall. It is visited by about 300,000 people each year.

Where are "The Streets of Laredo"?
The town brought to life in the 19th-century cowboy song of that name is located in Texas.

Who is the city of Seattle named for?
It is named for a local Indian chief, whose name was variously spelled Seattle, See-yat, and Sealth.

What does the name "Alaska" mean?
It comes from an Aleutian word meaning "mainland," distinguishing it from the islands on which the Aleutian people lived.

Where did "Storyville" get its name?
The fabled district of New Orleans got its name from Alderman Sidney Story, who, in 1897, moved the city's illegal activities—such as gambling and prostitution—into a restricted district along Basin Street, next to the French Quarter. Storyville flourished until 1917, when the secretary of the Navy had it closed down to protect the troops from vice.

What city was the focus of Robert and Helen Lynd's *Middletown* studies?
The revealing 1929 study, *Middletown: A Study in Contemporary American Culture*, examined family life in Muncie, Indiana. It was followed by *Middletown in Transition* in 1937.

What states are part of the Tennessee Valley?
There are seven: Alabama, Georgia, Kentucky, Mississippi, North Carolina, Tennessee, and Virginia. The valley of the Tennessee River and its tributaries encompasses 41,000 square miles, with the largest part in Tennessee. The Tennessee Valley Authority (TVA) was created in 1933 to control floods, improve navigation, and bring low-cost electrical power to the entire area.

What states comprised the Dust Bowl?
The Dust Bowl was the name given to the region of the Great

Plains wracked by drought in 1934–37 during the Great Depression. It contained portions of several states, including Oklahoma, Texas, Colorado, Kansas, and New Mexico.

What was the first all-Federal housing project in America?
It was an eleven-block, low-rent housing project called Techwood, in Atlanta, Georgia. Built in 1936 by the Public Works Administration, it cost $2,875,000. The project offered 22 brick-and-concrete apartments for families with annual incomes under $1,800.

What were the main businesses in Las Vegas before it became a center for gambling?
The town was a sparsely populated mining and ranching community. Gambling did take place in the town throughout most of its history, but Las Vegas did not become known as a mecca for gambling until after the Flamingo Hotel was opened in 1946 by gangster Benjamin "Bugsy" Siegel.

For whom was Levittown named?
It was named for the construction company that designed and built the post-World War II suburban developments–Levitt and Sons, William Levitt, owner. The first Levittown development was built between 1947–51 in Hempstead, New York.

How many Levittowns were built in the post–World War II era?
There were three pioneering suburban housing developments bearing the Levittown name: the one in Hempstead, New York, in the late 1940s; one near Philadelphia in the 1950s; and one in New Jersey in the 1960s.

When is the Tulip Festival held in Holland, Michigan?
The annual Tulip Time Festival, featuring Dutch food, entertainment, and parades, has been held during mid-May in this mostly

Dutch-American community since 1929. Former Presidents Ford, Reagan, and Bush have all taken part in the festivities.

How much did a night in a New York hotel cost fifty years ago?
In 1939, a night at the Essex House on Central Park South cost $6. Today, a night in the same hotel starts at $185.

Sports

What was the first American book written about baseball?
It was the *Book of Sports* by Robin Carver, published in 1834.

When was the National Baseball Hall of Fame dedicated?
It was dedicated in 1939 at Cooperstown, New York, to honor the centennial of the alleged invention of baseball by Army officer Abner Doubleday at Cooperstown in 1839. However, it was later proven that Doubleday was not even at Cooperstown in 1839 (he was a cadet at West Point) and that the word "baseball" was used as early as the 18th century to refer to American and British ancestors of the modern game. Credit for the codification of modern baseball rules now usually goes to Alexander Cartwright and the Knickerbocker Club of New York in 1845.

When was "The Star-Spangled Banner" first played at a sporting event?
It was played in 1862 at a baseball game in Brooklyn at a field built by sports developer William Commeyer.

At what baseball game did TV star Roseanne Arnold make an obscene gesture to cap her rendition of the national anthem?
The comedienne made headlines for her performance at the July 25, 1990, game of the San Diego Padres-Cincinnati Reds. Arnold

grabbed her crotch in response to boos at her handling of the anthem.

What was the first American college football game?
It took place on November 6, 1869, in New Brunswick, New Jersey. Rutgers beat Princeton, six goals to four. The rules used were actually those for soccer. It was not until the 1870s that rugby rules began to prevail in the sport, making the game more like modern football.

When was the first Kentucky Derby?
The initial jewel in the Triple Crown was first held in 1875 at Churchill Downs.

What three horse races make up the Triple Crown?
The Kentucky Derby, the Preakness (begun at Pimlico, Baltimore, in 1873), and the Belmont (begun in 1867 at Jerome Park, New York; now held in Belmont Park, New York).

What horse first won the Triple Crown?
Sir Barton in 1919.

Where was the first baseball game played under electric lights?
Electric lights were first used for a baseball game between Fort Wayne and Indianapolis teams on May 28, 1883, in Fort Wayne, Indiana.

Where was James Naismith teaching when he invented basketball?
The YMCA Training College, now Springfield College, in Springfield, Massachusetts. Naismith invented the game for his students in the winter of 1891–92 to provide indoor exercise between the football and baseball seasons.

When was the National League formed?
The baseball league was formed in 1876. Its charter members were Chicago, St. Louis, Hartford, Boston, Louisville, New York, Philadelphia, and Cincinnati.

What about the American League?
It was founded in 1900 and received major league status in 1901. Its charter members included Chicago, Boston, Detroit, Philadelphia, Washington, Cleveland, Milwaukee, and Baltimore.

Who played in the first World Series?
The first World Series between the American and National Leagues was played in 1903. The Boston Red Sox (AL) beat the Pittsburgh Pirates (NL) five games to three in a best-of-nine series.

When was the first Rose Bowl played?
The New Year's Day football game was first played between the University of Michigan and Stanford University in Pasadena, California, in 1902. Michigan won 49–0.

What was the first Olympics held in the United States?
The third Olympiad, held in St. Louis, Missouri, in 1904.

What positions did Tinker, Evers, and Chance play?
In the early 20th century, these three Chicago Cubs filled the following infield positions: Joe Tinker, shortstop; Johnny Evers, second base; Frank Chance, first base. Their fielding, immortalized in a popular sportswriter's phase, "Tinker-to-Evers-to-Chance," has become synonymous with crack teamwork.

What kind of car won the first Indianapolis 500?
A six-cylinder Marmon Wasp, driven by Ray Harroun at an av-

erage speed of 74.59 miles per hour, won the first 500-mile race at the Indianapolis Speedway in 1911.

What was Jim Thorpe's tribe?

The athlete's father was part Sac and Fox; his mother was part Potawatomi. Born at a Sac and Fox village in Oklahoma, Thorpe (1888–1953) won the pentathlon and decathlon at the 1912 Olympics and went on to play professional football and baseball. Although Thorpe was stripped of his gold medals for playing professional baseball before appearing in the Olympics, the medals were restored posthumously in 1982.

How much did the New York Yankees pay the Boston Red Sox for Babe Ruth?

In 1920, the Yankees paid $125,000 for the Babe.

What nationality was Jack Dempsey's contender in the Dempsey-Firpo heavyweight title fight of 1923?

The challenger Luis Firpo, known as the "Wild Bull of the Pampas," was Argentine. Dempsey defeated him in a brutal fight that ended less than a minute into the second round at New York's Polo Grounds on September 4, 1923. The event is immortalized in the 1924 painting by George Bellows, *The Dempsey-Firpo Fight,* which shows Dempsey being punched out of the ring before coming back to beat his opponent.

When did Gene Tunney beat Jack Dempsey for the heavyweight boxing championship?

James J. "Gene" Tunney sent Harrison "Jack" Dempsey against the ropes in 1926. Dempsey had held the title since 1919, when he defeated Jess Willard.

What was the first American city to be admitted to the National Hockey League?

Boston, in 1924. The Boston Bruins won their first Stanley Cup

Championship in 1929 and have won it five times since then
(1939, 1941, 1970, 1972, 1990).

How long has the Heisman Trophy been awarded?
It has been awarded since 1935 by the Downtown Athletic Club
of New York City to the country's top college football player.

**What college has generated the most winners of the Heisman
Trophy?**
Notre Dame holds the honor, with seven Heisman Trophy win-
ners:

    1943—Angelo Bertelli, quarterback
    1947—John Lujack, quarterback
    1949—Leon Hart, end
    1953—John Lattner, halfback
    1956—Paul Hornung, quarterback
    1964—John Huarte, quarterback
    1987—Tim Brown, wide receiver

**Who did Joe Louis beat to become the world heavyweight
champion?**
Born Joseph Louis Barrow (1914–83) near Lafayette, Louisiana,
the African-American boxer defeated James J. Braddock for the
championship on June 22, 1937. Known as the "Brown Bomber,"
Louis held the title for 12 years, from 1937 until he retired in
1949. During this period, he defended his title a record 25 times.

How many times did Joe Louis fight Max Schmeling?
Twice. In their first encounter in 1936, before Louis became
heavyweight champion, the German boxer emerged the win-
ner. In 1938, now the world champion, Louis beat Schmeling
in a one-round knockout that struck a symbolic blow to Nazi
Germany's claims of national and racial superiority. Louis's
initial loss to Schmeling was one of only three defeats (as

against 69 victories) in his career; the other two took place during a brief comeback attempt in 1950 and 1951.

What is Yogi Berra's real name?
He was born Lawrence Peter Berra in St. Louis, Missouri, in 1925. He joined the New York Yankees in 1946.

What is Casey Stengel's real name?
He was born Charles Dillon Stengel in Kansas City, Missouri (c. 1890–1975). Stengel managed the New York Yankees from 1949 to 1960 and the Mets from 1962 to 1965.

Who founded the National Association for Stock Car Auto Racing?
NASCAR, headquartered in Daytona Beach, Florida, was founded by William H. G. France in 1947.

How old was Satchel Paige when he signed to a major league team?
Forty-two-year-old Leroy "Satchel" Paige became the oldest rookie in pro baseball when he signed with the Cleveland Indians in 1948. He had been a pitcher in the Negro Leagues since 1926.

Where is the Pro Football Hall of Fame?
At the National Football Museum in Canton, Ohio.

Who hit the winning home run in the 1951 National League playoffs between the Brooklyn Dodgers and the New York Giants?
The winning home run was hit in the bottom of the ninth at the New York Polo Grounds by the Giants' third baseman Bobby Thomson. With two men on base, Thomson's home run changed the score from Dodgers 4, Giants 2, to Giants 5, Dodgers 4.

What male figure skater has most often won the U.S. Skating Championship?
As of 1992, the honor goes to Richard (Dick) Button, who held the title for seven years from 1946 to 1952. Four skaters have held the title for four years:

    Hayes Jenkins—1953–56
    David Jenkins—1957–60
    Scott Hamilton—1981–84
    Brian Boitano—1985–88

What female figure skater has most often won the U.S. Skating Championship?
As of 1992, the honor goes to Gretchen Merrill, who held the title for six years, from 1943 to 1948. Two women have held the title for five years:

    Tenley Albright—1952–56
    Peggy Fleming—1964–68

What was Hank Aaron's first major league team?
He entered the major leagues as right fielder with the Milwaukee Braves in 1954. He moved to Atlanta with the team in 1966. On April 8, 1974, he broke Babe Ruth's record for career home runs.

Who pitched the only perfect game in World Series history?
The no-hitter was pitched by Don Larsen of the New York Yankees against the Brooklyn Dodgers in the fifth game of the 1956 World Series.

Who was the first black professional hockey player?
Willie O'Ree, who played one season for the Boston Bruins, 1960–61.

Who was the first U.S. professional male golfer to win over $1 million during his career? The first female?
Arnold Palmer, in 1963. No U.S. professional female golfer earned this much money until Kathy Wentworth in 1981.

When did Cassius Clay announce that he had changed his name to Muhammad Ali?
In February 1964, after defeating Sonny Liston and becoming heavyweight champion. Some time earlier, Ali had secretly joined the Nation of Islam, led by Elijah Muhammad.

Who won the U.S.-U.S.S.R. Olympic basketball final in 1972?
At first, it seemed that the U.S. had won 50–49. But it was ruled that the clock was wrong, and there were three seconds left to play. When the teams resumed the game, the U.S.S.R. scored a basket to win 51–50. It was the first U.S. basketball title defeat in 36 years. The U.S. team refused to accept the silver medals.

What were the scores of the sets between Billie Jean King and Bobby Riggs during their "Battle of the Sexes"?
In the 1973 match between the former Wimbledon men's champion and the then-current Wimbledon women's champion, the 30-year old King defeated the 55-year old Riggs in three straight sets—6–4, 6–3, 6–3. Riggs had challenged King to a "Battle of the Sexes," claiming that despite their age difference he could beat King because she was a woman.

Who is the NBA lifetime leader in most games played?
Kareem Abdul-Jabbar, with 1,560 games. Born Ferdinand Lewis (Lew) Alcindor in 1947, Abdul-Jabbar began playing for the Milwaukee Bucks in 1969 and the Los Angeles Lakers in 1975.

Who are the top three leading NFL touchdown scorers?
As of 1991, they are:

Jim Brown—126 touchdowns
Walter Payton—125 touchdowns
John Riggins—116 touchdowns

From what part of Brooklyn do Mike Tyson and Riddick Bowe hail?

Both Mike Tyson, 1986 and 1987 Heavyweight World Champion, and Riddick Bowe, 1992 Heavyweight World Champion, are from Brownsville.

Where did Pete Rose serve his prison term?

Beginning in August 1990, baseball's hits leader served a five-month term at the federal prison at Marion, Illinois, for income tax evasion. In August 1989, baseball commissioner Bart Giamatti had banned Rose from baseball for alleged gambling on major league games.

What are the most popular U.S. spectator sports?

Major league baseball is the most popular, with about 56.6 million fans in attendance in 1990. Thoroughbred racing is close behind, with attendance of about 56.2 million. Basketball and football are far behind, with only about 16 million fans attending games in 1990.

How many times was Magic Johnson named the NBA's Most Valuable Player?

Three times, in 1987, 1989, and 1990. Earvin "Magic" Johnson retired from pro basketball after announcing that he had the AIDS virus in November 1991.

For how long was Mike Ditka the coach of the Chicago Bears?

For 11 seasons. He took over as coach in 1982 and was relieved of his position in January 1993, at the close of the 1992 season. He led the Bears to victory in the 1986 Super Bowl.

What is the average annual salary of a major league baseball player?
In 1992, it was $1,014,947. Currently, the highest paid player is Barry Bonds of the San Francisco Giants at $7.3 million.

When was the first Super Bowl played in the Louisiana Superdome?
Super Bowl XII was played in the Superdome in New Orleans on January 15, 1978. Dallas beat Denver 27 to 10. The largest arena in human history, the Superdome covers 13 acres and reaches a height of 27 stories.

When did Oriole Park at Camden Yards open?
The traditional baseball-only park opened in Baltimore in April 1992. Influenced by big-league parks of the early 1900s like Ebbets Field, Fenway Park, and Wrigley Field, Oriole Park has an assymetrical playing field and natural grass turf. Its location, Camden Yards, was an important railroad center and in the mid-19th century a stop for the transportation of slaves through the Underground Railroad.

Statistics

What percentage of Americans were farmers in Revolutionary War times? At the end of World War II? Today?
During the Revolutionary War years, 90 percent of Americans were farmers. By World War II, the number had shrunk to 15 percent. Today fewer than 3 percent of the population are farmers.

What is the most hated food in the United States?
In a 1992 Gallup Poll, 14 percent of Americans said they hated liver the most. Tied for second place in the worst foods list were spinach, fish, and seafood, each at 6 percent.

What percentage of Americans consider themselves politically moderate?
Forty-two percent classify themselves this way, according to a 1992 *New York Times*/CBS News Poll.

What percentage of the nation's reporters are Democrats?
44.4 percent of American newspaper, radio, and television journalists identify themselves that way, according to a 1992 survey by the nonpartisan Freedom Forum.

What percentage are Republicans?
16.3 percent. 34.4 percent are independents.

What are the top ten religious denominations in the United States?

According to a study by the Association of Statisticians of American Religious Bodies, they are (with number of members in millions):

1. Roman Catholic	53.4
2. Southern Baptist Convention	18.9
3. United Methodist	11.1
4. Black Baptist	8.7
5. Jewish	6.0
6. Evangelical Lutheran Church in America	5.2
7. Presbyterian	3.6
8. Church of Jesus Christ of Latter-Day Saints	3.5
9. Lutheran Church-Missouri Synod	2.6
10. Episcopal	2.4

How tall is the average American?

According to the National Center for Health Statistics, the average male is 5 feet 9.1 inches tall. The average female is 5 feet 3.7 inches tall.

What is the median age in the United States?

It was 33 in 1990.

What was the racial breakdown of the U.S. population at the beginning of the 20th century?

Of 76 million Americans, 87 percent were white, 11.4 percent were black, and nearly 2 percent were "other."

At the present day?

According to the 1990 census, of 248.7 million Americans, 80.3 percent are white, 12.1 percent are black, and nearly 8 percent are "other." Asians and Pacific Islanders now represent 2.9 percent of the population, compared to less than 1 percent in 1900.

What is the poorest county in the United States?
It is Shannon County, South Dakota, site of the Pine Ridge Reservation, which is home to the Oglala branch of the Sioux Indians. In 1987, 63.1 percent of all 9,900 residents here lived in poverty, compared to a national poverty rate of 13.5 percent.

What U.S. county has the lowest poverty rate?
Loving, Texas, population 107, with a poverty rate of zero in 1989. Ozaukee, Wisconsin (population 72,800), is close behind, with a poverty rate of 2.2 percent.

How typical is the American nuclear family, with two parents and their children living together?
Not very, according to an analysis of 1990 census data by the Center for the Study of Social Policy. The most common type of household in the United States is a married couple without children: There are 27.5 million of these. In second place (at 26.9 million) are nonfamily households of unrelated individuals. In third place are the 24.2 million households with parents and children.

> *How many American children live in a two-parent family where one parent works and the other stays home?*
> Only one in four.

What percentage of the U.S. population aged 25 and over has completed high school?
In 1989, the total was 76.9 percent.

> *What percentage has completed college?*
> Only 21.1 percent.

How many Americans are employed in the health care industry?
Ten million Americans were employed in the health care field in

1992, an increase of 43 percent in four years. This vigorous growth contrasts with an increase of only 1 percent in private employment overall during the same period. The Commerce Department expects health spending in the U.S. to exceed $1 trillion in 1994.

What percentage of American households have a TV set?
In 1992, 98 percent of U.S. households had a TV set. Sixty-five percent had two or more.

   What percentage have videocassette recorders?
   Seventy-seven percent.

How much television does the average American watch?
Nielsen Media Services reported in 1990–91 that the average American (older than one year) watches 28 hours 13 minutes of television per week—about four hours per day.

How much credit card debt does the average American owe?
The average credit card holder owes $2,317 on credit cards, according to the Nilson Report, Santa Monica, California. About 60 percent of American adults own at least one credit card.

How much garbage does the average American generate?
Three pounds per day, according to the Garbage Project.

Trademarks

What does A&P stand for?
The name is an abbreviation for the Great Atlantic and Pacific Tea Company. One of the nation's top grocery chains, it was founded in New York in 1859 by George Huntington Harford and George P. Gilman as the Great American Tea Company. It was renamed in 1869 to take advantage of national interest in the transcontinental railroad.

Who founded the Standard Oil Company?
It wasn't only John D. Rockefeller. What would become the country's largest oil company was founded in 1867 by four people—Rockefeller, Henry M. Flagler, S. V. Harkness, and Rockefeller's brother William.

When did A. G. Spalding start selling sporting goods?
Albert Goodwill Spalding (1850–1915) co-founded the sporting goods firm "A. G. Spalding and Brothers" in 1876. Born in Byron, Illinois, Spalding pitched for Boston and Chicago and helped to found the National League.

When did Bloomingdale's open?
The New York City department store owned by Lyman, Joseph, and Gustave Bloomingdale opened in 1886 at Third Avenue and

59th Street, near a station of the Third Avenue El. By 1927, Bloomingdale's occupied the entire block, where it is located to this day.

Which is older, Coca-Cola or Pepsi-Cola?

Coca-Cola, by ten years. It was introduced to the American public in 1886, Pepsi-Cola in 1896.

> *What size bottle did they come in?*
> For decades, Coca-Cola was sold in a six-and-one-half-ounce bottle. Depending on the bottler, Pepsi-Cola came in six, six-and-one-half, and seven-ounce sizes. Starting in 1934, however, Pepsi was sold in 12-ounce bottles, but for the same price as the smaller Coke—five cents. The bargain that Pepsi offered was highlighted in a 1939 radio jingle: "Pepsi-Cola hits the spot/Twelve full ounces, that's a lot/Twice as much for a nickel, too/Pepsi-Cola is the drink for you."

What was the first product sold by Sears and Roebuck?

Merchant Richard Sears and watchmaker Alvah C. Roebuck began their collaboration in 1887 by selling mail-order watches advertised in newspapers. In 1889, Sears produced his first catalogue of watches and other jewelry. By 1893, when the name Sears, Roebuck & Co. was first used, the business included clothing, furniture, baby carriages, and more. A century later, in 1993, it was announced that the general catalogue would cease publication.

When was the first Kodak camera sold?

George Eastman, a New York bank clerk, developed the first hand-held roll-film camera in 1888. The cost was $25.

When was the first American Express Travelers' Cheque issued?

In 1891. Then as now, Travelers' Cheques were designed to allow travelers to carry funds safely. American Express levied a surcharge on buyers of the cheques and paid banks a commission for each sale.

When was Jell-O invented?
In the mid-1890s, Mr. and Mrs. Pearl B. Wait of LeRoy, New York, adapted a gelatin dessert that had been patented by inventor Peter Cooper and named it Jell-O. In 1899, the Waits sold the business to Francis Woodward, founder of the Genessee Pure Food Company. By 1906, Woodward had sold $1 million worth of Jell-O. In 1925, Jell-O was one of the companies that formed the conglomerate General Foods.

When were Tinkertoys invented?
In 1913, Illinois stonemason Charles Pajean brought the toy he created for his children to the American Toy Fair in New York City. Within one year, 1 million Tinkertoy sets had been sold.

What was the Toll House behind the chocolate-chip cookies known as Toll House cookies?
It was a Massachusetts eatery called the Toll House Restaurant, run by Ruth Wakefield, who popularized the cookies in the early 20th century. She later sold the rights to the name "Toll House Cookies" to the Nestlé Company.

When did J. P. Morgan organize the U.S. Steel Corporation?
In 1901, John Pierpont Morgan financed the merger that resulted in the formation of U.S. Steel, the first billion-dollar company.

What was the original name of the Xerox Corporation?
From 1906 to 1960 it was known as the Haloid Company, headquartered in New York. In 1961 it became the Xerox Corporation.

What was the original name of IBM?
The company now known as International Business Machines was originally founded as the Computing Tabulating Recording Company in 1911.

When did Henry Ford found the Ford Motor Company?
In 1903 in Detroit, Michigan.

When did William C. Durant found the General Motors Corporation?
In 1908, in Flint, Michigan.

What car was known as the Tin Lizzie? The Flivver?
Both were nicknames for the Model T, introduced by Henry Ford in 1908.

How many Model Ts were sold?
About 15 million.

When did Filene's Basement open?
Filene's Automatic Bargain Basement opened in the Boston flagship store in 1909. It followed the first example of bargain basements—the "Bargain Room" at Wanamaker's in Philadelphia.

Who invented Betty Crocker?
The name was created by the Washburn Crosby Company (a forerunner of General Mills) in 1921 to be used in response to letters and recipe requests from homemakers. In 1924, Betty's voice was first heard on the Betty Crocker "Cooking School of the Air," the first food service program on daytime radio. Not until 1936 did Betty have a face: that was when her first official portrait was commissioned. The portrait has been redone five times since then, to reflect changing images of the American woman.

Which canning company invented the Jolly Green Giant?
The Minnesota Valley Canning Company of Le Sueur, Minnesota, introduced the Jolly Green Giant as the emblem of a line of canned peas in 1926.

When did Woolworth's start offering products that cost more than five or ten cents?
In 1932, the Woolworth chain of "five & dime" stores began to offer 20-cent merchandise in addition to five- and ten-cent items.

Where was Ragú founded?
Famed for its Italian flavors, the Ragú line of products was founded in Rochester, New York, in 1937 by two Italian immigrants, Giovanni and Assunta Contisano. Ragú became the first nationally distributed brand of pasta sauce in the U.S. in 1989, after it was acquired by Chesebrough-Pond's.

Who was the original voice of "Speedy," the Alka-Seltzer puppet?
Dick Beals, himself only four-and-a-half feet tall, did the voice of the singing animated puppet in over 200 TV commercials from 1954 to 1964. Speedy, who had an Alka-Seltzer tablet for a hat and another for his torso, was designed by Robert Watkins for Wade Advertising of Chicago.

Who invented the Frisbee?
Yale University students appear to have begun the game in the 1920s, when they threw around metal pie tins from the Frisbie Bakery of Bridgeport, Connecticut. (Middlebury College in Vermont has also taken credit for inventing the game.) As a commercial venture, however, Frisbee began with a saucer-shaped toy invented by Walter Frederick Morrison in the 1950s. The Wham-O company of California introduced it in 1957 as the Pluto Platter; the name was changed to Frisbee in 1959.

When were the first pantyhose introduced?
In 1959, Glen Raven Mills of North Carolina brought out Panti-Legs, the first pantyhose. Allen Grant, president of Glen Raven, got the idea when his wife Ethel complained about the discomfort of nylon stockings and garter belts.

How big was the original G.I. Joe?
The original "action figure," introduced in 1964 by Hassenfeld Bros. (later Hasbro) of Newport, Rhode Island, was 12 inches tall. By 1982, G.I. Joe had shrunk down to three inches.

Who is credited with inventing the miniskirt?
Mary Quant, co-owner (with her husband Alexander Plunket Greene) of the boutique Bazaar in Chelsea, London. Quant, "the mother of the miniskirt," premiered the new fashion item at Bazaar in 1965.

When was Diners Club introduced?
The first credit card for buying goods and services from more than one institution was invented in 1950 by Frank McNamara. McNamara, a loan company executive in New York, got the idea when he found himself short of money at a restaurant.

When were MasterCard and Visa introduced?
Visa began in 1965 as the Bank of America's BankAmericard, backed by a group of banks able to exchange funds nationally. It received its current name, Visa, in 1977, to promote its international image and acknowledge the cooperation of banks in other countries. MasterCard began in 1966 as the Interbank card issued by another consortium of banks. It became Master Charge in 1969 and MasterCard in 1979.

When did Diet Coke first appear on the U.S. market?
The original Diet Coke, made with saccharin, debuted in July

1982. An updated version of Diet Coke, made with NutraSweet, first appeared in August 1983.

Where was the original McDonald's located?
Richard and Maurice McDonald opened their original drive-in stand in San Bernardino, California, in 1940. Beginning in 1948, they switched to a new streamlined system, with a limited menu, low prices, fast service, and disposable wrappings. In 1954, milk-shake machine salesman Ray Kroc became the franchising agent for the successful restaurant idea. Six years later, Kroc bought all rights to the business.

How many McDonald's hamburgers are made from a pound of meat?
Ten per pound, apportioned by a computer formula.

Women's History

Who was the first known suffragette in American history?
Margaret Brent, who demanded the right to vote in Maryland's colonial assembly in 1647.

Why is the name "Mary Katherine Goddard" on some early copies of the Declaration of Independence?
She published the first official copies of the Declaration—the first to bear the names of all the signers—in January 1777. At the time, Goddard was the only printer in Baltimore, where the Continental Congress had fled from Philadelphia. She had taken over the print shop and the city's only newspaper from her brother William while he was in debtor's prison. Mary Goddard went on to serve as Baltimore's first postmaster from 1775 to 1789—making her the first woman to hold a federal position.

What was the first women's college in America? The first coeducational college?
The first women's college was the Troy Female Seminary, in Troy, New York, founded by Emma Willard (1787–1870) in 1821. The first coeducational college was Oberlin College, which first accepted female students in 1833.

When did abortion become illegal throughout much of the United States?
Most states outlawed or restricted abortion during the period

1830–1880. Before then, abortion in the first months of pregnancy (until "quickening", or the first perception of fetal movement) was legal throughout most of the country in keeping with colonial common law. The drive to prohibit abortion came from a variety of sources, including the desire of the medical profession to regulate surgical procedures, concern about falling birth rates, and reaction to the women's rights movement.

How old was Margaret Fuller when she became editor of the *Dial*?
The feminist writer was 30 when Ralph Waldo Emerson asked her to edit his Transcendentalist periodical in 1840. During her life she also worked as the foreign correspondent for the *New York Tribune* and wrote the influential collection of essays, *Woman in the Nineteenth Century* (1845), which served as an inspiration for the Women's Rights Convention at Seneca Falls, New York, in 1848.

Who was the first woman in the U.S. to receive an M.D. degree?
Elizabeth Blackwell (1821–1910). She received her degree in 1849 from Geneva Medical College in New York.

How many black women attended the first National Woman's Rights Convention?
Only one—itinerant preacher and abolitionist Sojourner Truth. The convention was held in Worcester, Massachusetts, in 1850.

What did bloomers have to do with female independence?
Consisting of a belted tunic that reached just below the knees and baggy trousers gathered at the ankles, this garment was introduced in 1851 by American feminist Amelia Jenks Bloomer. She considered it a lighter, less confining costume for active women than the heavy hoop skirts of the day. Originally designed by Bloomer's friend Elizabeth Miller, the garment was popularized in

Bloomer's newspaper, the *Lily,* the first women's journal to be produced by a woman. The word "bloomers" was coined by critics as a term of derision; it eventually became the name of an undergarment of similar design.

Did Susan B. Anthony ever vote in an election?

The women's rights leader (1820–1906) did not live to see the 19th Amendment adopted in 1920 guaranteeing women the right to vote. But Anthony had voted illegally in a Rochester, New York, election in 1872, and refused to pay the fine that followed.

When was the starting point of the 20-year period described by Jane Addams in *Twenty Years at Hull-House?*

The score of years began in 1889 when Addams (1860–1935) and her friend Ellen Starr moved into an old mansion in a poor neighborhood of Chicago. Hull-House became a center for social and political activism. In 1910, Addams published her autobiography—*Twenty Years at Hull-House.* She remained at the settlement until the end of her life.

Who was the first woman formally nominated for the U.S. presidency?

It was Belva Ann Lockwood (1830–1917), feminist and lawyer, who was nominated in 1884 and 1888 as the candidate of the National Equal Rights Party. An advocate of equal rights for women and international peace, Lockwood was also the first woman admitted to practice law before the U.S. Supreme Court.

What part did Clara Maass play in the battle against yellow fever?

After serving in the Spanish-American War, New Jersey nurse Clara Maass volunteered in 1901 to take part in yellow fever experiments in Cuba. Dr. Walter Reed designed the experiments to see whether a mild case of the disease would render people immune. Maass allowed herself to be bitten twice by infected mosquitoes. She developed not a mild case but a mortal one that killed her at age 25. Her sacrifice is remembered in the name of the Clara Maass Memorial Hospital in New Jersey.

Who coined the term "birth control"?
Margaret Sanger (1883–1966) in 1914. Sanger founded the first birth control clinic in the U.S., in 1916. In 1921, she established the American Birth Control League, predecessor to the Planned Parenthood Federation.

Who was the first woman elected to Congress?
Jeannette Rankin (1880–1973) was elected as Montana's sole delegate to the House of Representatives in 1916. After serving her term, she was not reelected until 1940. A pacifist, she holds the distinction of being the only member of Congress to have voted against American participation in both World Wars.

Who was the first woman elected to the U.S. Senate?
Hattie T. Caraway, a Democrat from Arkansas, was elected to the Senate in 1932.

When was the League of Women Voters founded?
It was founded in Chicago in 1920 by Carrie Chapman Catt, along with other leaders of the National American Woman Suffrage Association. Its aim was to strengthen the political power of women following passage of the 19th Amendment (granting women the vote). Since then, the organization's aims broadened to general advocacy for social and political reform.

Can men be members?
Yes, since 1974.

Why did anthropologist Margaret Mead (1901–78) choose to study Samoa?
There were several practical reasons why the young Columbia

graduate student decided to do field work on Samoan adolescence. She thought her fluency in French and German would help her in the Polynesian island chain, and there were regular steamship stops there. More important, she wanted to know how much of human behavior was culturally induced as opposed to biologically based. As she later said, "One of the jobs of the anthropologist is to get people to see that many of the things that we think of as universal were only invented yesterday and don't fit anymore today." Mead's first book, *Coming of Age in Samoa,* was published in 1928.

What was the intended destination of Amelia Earhart on her final flight?
On the July 2, 1938, flight during which she disappeared, the aviatrix was traveling from New Guinea to Howland Island, in the Pacific. In June 1928, Earhart had become the first woman to fly across the Atlantic, one year after Charles Lindbergh's transatlantic flight. Earhart's remains were never found.

What organization blocked the performance of Marian Anderson at Washington D.C.'s Constitution Hall?
The Daughters of the American Revolution refused to rent Constitution Hall to contralto Anderson for a concert in 1938 because she was black. Appalled by this action, First Lady Eleanor Roosevelt, a DAR member, resigned from the organization and rallied support in Anderson's behalf. Later that year, Roosevelt was able to arrange a performance for Anderson at the Lincoln Memorial. It was attended by 75,000 people.

When was the National Organization for Women founded?
The women's rights group was founded in 1966 by Betty Friedan, author of the 1963 book, *The Feminine Mystique.*

Who was the first black woman elected to Congress?
It was Brooklyn-born Shirley Chisholm (1924–   ), who was

elected to Congress from that borough in 1969. In 1972, she ran unsuccessfully for the Democratic nomination for president.

Who was the "Roe" in Roe v. Wade?
The woman who sued the state of Texas for denying her the right to abort a fetus was named Norma McGorvey. In 1973, the Supreme Court ruled 7-2 that women had the right to abort a fetus during the first trimester of pregnancy.

Who wrote the majority opinion in that case?
Justice Harry Blackmun. Justices William Rehnquist and Byron White dissented.

What company is the world's largest employer of women?
It is Avon Products, Inc., which, as of 1992, employed 1.5 million women throughout the world. Nearly all the women work as independent sales representatives, often known as Avon ladies. Founded in 1883 by David H. McConnell as the California Perfume Company, it became Avon Products, Inc. in 1939, a decade after a line of household and personal care products were introduced under the name Avon.

By how many states did the Equal Rights Amendment elude ratification?
Three. Between 1972 and 1982, 35 state legislatures approved the amendment. Thirty-eight were needed for the amendment to be incorporated into the Constitution.

Where did *Our Bodies, Ourselves* get its name?
The 1973 women's health sourcebook stems from a 1969 course created in Boston by a group of women (now known as the Boston Women's Health Book Collective). As their course about women and their bodies evolved, so did the title. Originally titled *Women and their Bodies,* it became the more inclusive *Women and*

Our Bodies, and finally *Our Bodies, Ourselves.* The book was revised in 1984 and 1992.

How do women's wages compare to men's wages?
According to median income figures for 1990, women with four years of college make 72 percent of what their male counterparts make. Women who are high school graduates make 67 percent of what their male counterparts make.

World War II

How long did the attack on Pearl Harbor last?
The surprise Japanese attack on the U.S. naval base in Hawaii began at 7:55 A.M. local time on December 7, 1941, and lasted nearly two hours. Over 2,300 Americans were killed; an additional 1,100 were wounded. More than ten ships were sunk or severely damaged; more than 140 aircraft were destroyed.

How many men took part in Lieutenant Colonel James Doolittle's 1942 raid on Tokyo?
Eighty men, aboard 16 B-25 Mitchell bombers, took part in the raid on April 18, 1942. Launched from the carrier USS *Hornet,* the planes bombed five Japanese cities: Tokyo, Yokohama, Kobe, Nagoya, and Osaka. The raid rattled the Japanese and boosted American morale at a time when Japan seemed invincible.

Where is Bataan?
The Bataan Peninsula is in the Philippines. Following the Allied surrender of Bataan to the Japanese in April 1942, it was the site of the infamous "death march" in which thousands of American and Filipino prisoners died.

How many shells did warships fire at the Battle of Midway?
None. The decisive Allied victory on June 4, 1942, was significant

in naval history because the two opposing fleets never fired at or even came in view of each other. The Japanese and American fleets attacked each other with submarines and planes launched from aircraft carriers. American planes sank all four Japanese aircraft carriers, repelling a Japanese assault on Midway island northwest of Hawaii. One American carrier, the *Yorktown,* was lost.

How long did it take American forces to capture Guadalcanal Island?

Six months, from the landing of the First Marine Division on August 7, 1942, to the evacuation of the last Japanese on February 8, 1943. In the fighting, the Japanese lost about 10,000 men, the Americans about 1,600.

What was Operation Torch?

It was the Allied invasion of French North Africa beginning on November 8, 1942. Assault troops, almost all American, captured Morocco and Algiers with mostly British naval support.

Which Aleutian Islands were occupied by the Japanese?

Japan occupied the islands Attu, Agattu, and Kiska from 1942 to 1943. The islands lie west of the Alaskan Peninsula.

How many internment camps were built to house Japanese-Americans during World War II?

In 1942, about 100,000 Japanese-Americans were moved to ten internment camps in Arkansas, Arizona, California, Colorado, Idaho, Utah, and Wyoming. The camps were closed in late 1945.

What World War II general was known as the "soldiers' general"?

Omar Bradley (1893–1981) earned this nickname for his unassuming manner and his concern for the welfare of soldiers.

What were the names of the two U.S. beachheads at Normandy in the D-Day invasion?
Omaha Beach and Utah Beach. The beachheads were secured in the invasion of June 6, 1944.

How many American women were employed during World War II?
The female work force grew from 11 million to approximately 20 million during the war.

How much money was raised from war bonds during World War II?
The seven bond drives, often led by top movie celebrities, yielded $61 billion. Among the more popular celebrity bond spokespersons were Bob Hope and Marlene Dietrich.

When and where did American forces meet Russian forces during the invasion of Germany in World War II?
The two Allied armies met on April 25, 1945, on the Elbe River at the town of Torgau. The Americans had been advancing from the west and the Russians from the east.

What was the most damaging air attack of World War II?
It was not the atomic bombing of Hiroshima but the firebombing of Tokyo by 279 Superfortress bombers on March 9–10, 1945. Over 1,650 tons of incendiary bombs were dropped on the city, raising a massive firestorm and killing from 80,000 to 120,000 people. The bombing represented a new tactic by American General Curtis LeMay, who was unsatisfied with the results of "precision bombing" of military targets and wanted to switch to night attacks on cities with firebombs.

Where is Yalta?
The Soviet port in the Crimea (now part of Ukraine) was the site of the February 1945 meeting of Roosevelt, Churchill, and Stalin.

Where is Potsdam?
The setting of the July 1945 meeting between Truman, Churchill, and Stalin is near Berlin, Germany.

Who took the famous photograph of the marines raising the American flag at Iwo Jima?

Associated Press photographer Joe Rosenthal took the picture of marines raising the flag on Mount Suribachi. The island of Iwo Jima spanned only eight square miles, but was strategically important for its closeness to Japan and hence its value as an air base. About 6,800 marines were killed and more than 18,200 wounded in the fighting from February 19 to March 17, 1945.

How many days passed between the dropping of the atomic bombs and V-J day?

Japan surrendered on August 15, 1945, six days after Nagasaki was bombed on August 9 and nine days after Hiroshima was bombed on August 6.

Trick Questions and Popular Delusions

What day was the official signing ceremony for the Declaration of Independence?
August 2, 1776—not July 4. On July 4, Congress approved the final draft of the declaration, and John Hancock and the secretary of the Congress signed it. But most members of Congress signed it at the official ceremony on August 2. A few signed it later than that; one did not get around to it until 1781.

Who rode from Boston to Concord on the night of April 18, 1775, with the news that the British were coming?
Not Paul Revere. Revere started on the journey, along with William Dawes and Samuel Prescott, but Dawes and Revere were stopped by a British patrol. Only Prescott actually made it to Concord.

What is the number of Supreme Court justices specified in the U.S. Constitution?
No number is specified. The Supreme Court began with six justices, rose to a peak of ten during the Lincoln years, and settled at nine in 1869.

Who was the first president of the United States?
Technically, it was not George Washington, but John Hanson of

Maryland. In 1781, Hanson began a one-year term as the first "president of the United States in Congress assembled" under the Articles of Confederation. Seven other men served as president before Washington—technically, the ninth president—took office in 1789 under the new Constitution.

How do you spell the name of the inventor of the Derringer?
His name was Henry Deringer, Jr., (1786–1868), spelled with one "r". The Philadelphia gunsmith started making pistols in 1825 and came to specialize in the short-barreled, large-caliber pistol that bears his name. The extra "r" was added to "Derringer" by an imitator making similar pistols, and that became the accepted spelling.

From what law school did Clarence Darrow graduate?
None. Darrow (1857–1938), famed for his defense in the Scopes trial of 1925, briefly attended the University of Michigan law school but did not get a degree. He studied on his own and got most of his legal education in a law office in Youngstown, Ohio.

What ironclad ship fought the *Monitor* during the Civil War?
It was not called the *Merrimac*. The Union ship *Merrimac* had been renamed the *Virginia* by the Confederates. The *Virginia* fought the Union ironclad *Monitor* at Hampton Roads, Virginia, on March 9, 1862. The battle ended in a draw.

When was Adlai Stevenson vice-president of the U.S.?
The grandfather and namesake of 1950s Democratic Presidential candidate Adlai Stevenson served as vice-president from 1893 to 1897 under Grover Cleveland.

When did Oliver Wendell Holmes serve as chief justice of the Supreme Court?
He never did. He was an associate justice from 1902 to 1932, during the terms of four different chief justices.

What GM chairman said, "What's good for General Motors is good for the country"?
No GM chairman ever said it. The line actually was, "What's good for the country, is good for General Motors, and vice-versa," and it was said by Charles Wilson, a former GM head who was at the time the secretary of defense under President Eisenhower.

Who wrote *PT-109*?
The 1961 book about John F. Kennedy's exploits in World War II was written not by Kennedy but by Robert F. Donovan.

What was the first name of the federal official named Nixon whom the U.S. Senate impeached?
Walter. Walter L. Nixon, Jr., a judge of the U.S. District Court for Mississippi, was removed from office on November 3, 1989, after appearing before the Senate in its role as court of impeachment. President Richard Nixon resigned from office in August 1974 before the criminal proceeding known as impeachment could begin.

Bibliography

Archer, Jules. *The Incredible Sixties.* San Diego, CA: Harcourt Brace Jovanovich, 1986.

Asimov, Isaac. *Asimov's Chronology of Science & Discovery.* New York, NY: Harper & Row, 1989.

Beard, James. *James Beard's American Cookery.* Boston, MA: Little, Brown and Company, 1972.

Benét's Reader's Encyclopedia. New York, NY: Harper & Row, 1987.

Bennett, Lerone, Jr. *Before the Mayflower: A History of Black America,* 5th ed. New York, NY: Penguin Books, 1984.

Bines, Jonathan, et al. *Bushisms.* New York, NY: Workman, 1992.

Boller, Jr., Paul F. and John George. *They Never Said It.* New York, NY: Oxford University Press, 1989.

Braden, Donna. *Leisure and Entertainment in America.* Dearborn, MI: Henry Ford Museum & Greenfield Village, 1988.

Brooks, Tim and Earle Marsh. *The Complete Directory to Prime Time Network TV Shows: 1946–Present.* New York, NY: Ballantine, 1985.

Carruth, Gorton and associates, ed. *The Encyclopedia of American Facts and Dates,* 6th ed. New York, NY: Thomas Y. Crowell Co., 1972.

Catton, Bruce. *This Hallowed Ground.* New York, NY: Washington Square Press, 1961.

Cray, Ed, Jonathan Kotler, and Miles Beller. *American Datelines*. New York, NY: Facts On File, 1990.

Davis, Kenneth C. *Don't Know Much About History*. New York, NY: Avon, 1990.

Debo, Angie. *A History of the Indians of the United States*. Norman, OK: University of Oklahoma Press, 1970.

Dinnerstein, Leonard, Roger L. Nichols, David M. Reimers. *Natives and Strangers: Ethnic Groups and the Building of America*. New York, NY: Oxford University Press, 1979.

Eagle/Walking Turtle. *Indian America: A Traveler's Companion*. Sante Fe, NM: John Muir Publications, 1989.

Evans, Sarah M. *Born for Liberty: A History of Women in America*. New York, NY: Free Press, 1989.

The Family Car Songbook. Philadelphia, PA: Running Press, 1983.

Foner, Eric and John A. Garraty, eds. *The Reader's Companion to American History*. Boston, MA: Houghton Mifflin, 1991.

Fussell, Paul. *Wartime: Understanding and Behavior in the Second World War*. New York, NY: Oxford University Press, 1989.

Garraty, John A. *1,001 Things Everyone Should Know About American History*. New York, NY: Doubleday, 1989.

Grolier's Academic American Encyclopedia, online edition. Danbury, CT: Grolier Electronic Publishing, 1992.

Grun, Bernard. *The Timetables of History,* updated ed. New York, NY: Touchstone, 1982.

Gutman, Herbert G., et al. *Who Built America?*, 2 vols. New York, NY: Pantheon Books, 1989, 1992.

Hawke, David Freeman. *Everyday Life in Early America*. New York, NY: Harper & Row, 1988.

Hendrickson, Robert. *The Henry Holt Encyclopedia of Word and Phrase Origins*. New York: Henry Holt, 1987.

Howe, Irving. *World of Our Fathers*. New York, NY: Schocken Books, 1989.

The Information Please Almanac 1990, 1993. Boston, MA: Houghton Mifflin, 1989, 1992.

Javna, John. *The Best of TV Sitcoms.* New York, NY: Harmony, 1988.

Jones, Evan. *American Food: The Gastronomic Story,* 2nd ed. New York, NY: Vintage, 1981.

Katz, Ephraim. *The Film Encyclopedia.* New York, NY: Perigee, 1979.

Krout, John A. and Arnold S. Rice. *HarperCollins College Outline: United States History from 1865,* 20th ed. New York, NY: HarperCollins, 1991.

Larkin, Jack. *The Reshaping of Everyday Life.* New York, NY: Harper & Row, 1988.

Levey, Judith S. and Agnes Greenhall, eds. *The Concise Columbia Encyclopedia.* New York, NY: Columbia University Press, 1983.

Mendenhall, John. *Character Trademarks.* San Francisco, CA: Chronicle Books, 1990.

Morison, Samuel Eliot. *The Great Explorers.* New York, NY: Oxford, 1978.

Morison, Samuel Eliot. *The Oxford History of the American People,* 3 vols. New York, NY: New American Library, 1972.

Newman, Gerald, ed. *The Concise Encyclopedia of Sports,* 2nd rev. ed. New York, NY: Franklin Watts, 1979.

Newsweek.

The New York Times.

1939 World's Fair: The World of Tomorrow. Schenectady, NY: John P. Papp Historical Publications, 1973.

Ochoa, George. *The Fall of Mexico City.* Englewood Cliffs, NJ: Silver Burdett Press, 1989.

Ochoa, George, *The Fall of Quebec and the French and Indian War.* Englewood Cliffs, NJ: Silver Burdett Press, 1990.

Ousby, Ian, ed. *The Cambridge Guide to Literature in English.* Cambridge, UK: Cambridge University Press, 1988.

Page One: Major Events 1920–87 as Presented in The New York Times. New York, NY: Times Books, 1987.

Panati, Charles. *Extraordinary Origins of Everyday Things.* New York, NY: Harper & Row, 1987.

Raven, Susan and Alison Weir. *Women of Achievement.* New York, NY: Harmony Books, 1981.

Ravitch, Diane, ed. *The American Reader.* New York, NY: HarperPerennial, 1991.

Reader's Digest.

Rice, Arnold S., John A. Krout, and C. M. Harris. *HarperCollins College Outline: United States History to 1877,* 8th ed. New York, NY: HarperPerennial, 1991.

Robbins, Michael. *Top 10 Almanac 1991.* New York, NY: Workman, 1991.

Scherman, David E. *Life Goes to War.* New York, NY: Wallaby/Simon & Schuster, 1977.

Schlereth, Thomas J. *Victorian America: Transformations in Everyday Life.* New York, NY: HarperPerennial, 1991.

Shenkman, Richard. *Legends, Lies & Cherished Myths of American History.* New York, NY: Harper & Row, 1988.

Shenkman, Richard and Kurt Reiger. *One-Night Stands with American History.* New York, NY: Quill/Morrow, 1980.

Smith, Carter, exec. ed. *American Historical Images on File: The Civil War.* New York, NY: Facts On File, 1989.

Smith, Carter, ed. *Battles in a New Land: A Sourcebook on Colonial America.* Brookfield, CT: Millbrook Press, 1991.

Spicer, Edward H. *A Short History of the Indians of the United States.* Malabar, FL: Robert E. Krieger, 1969.

Stern, Jane & Michael. *Jane & Michael Stern's Encyclopedia of Pop Culture.* New York, NY: HarperPerennial, 1992.

Strasser, Susan. *Never Done: A History of American Housework.* New York, NY: Pantheon, 1982.

Trager, James. *The People's Chronology,* rev. ed. New York, NY: Henry Holt, 1992.

Tuleja, Tad. *American History in 100 Nutshells.* New York, NY: Fawcett Columbine, 1992.

Urdang, Lawrence, ed. *The Timetables of American History.* New York, NY: Simon & Schuster, 1981.

Wallechinsky, David and Irving Wallace. *The People's Almanac.* Garden City, NY: Doubleday, 1975.

Wallechinsky, David, Irving Wallace, Amy Wallace. *The Book of Lists.* New York, NY: Morrow, 1977.

Weisberger, Bernard A., ed. *The WPA Guide to America.* New York, NY: Pantheon, 1985.

Wetterau, Bruce. *The New York Public Library Book of Chronologies.* New York, NY: Prentice Hall Press, 1990.

White, Jon Manchip. *Everyday Life of the North American Indians.* New York, NY: Dorset Press, 1979.

Wiley, Mason and Damien Bona. *Inside Oscar.* New York, NY: Ballantine Books, 1988.

The World Almanac and Book of Facts 1992. New York, NY: World Almanac, 1991.

Worth, Fred L. *The Presidential Quiz Book.* New York, NY: Bell, 1988.

The WPA Guide to New York City. New York, NY: Pantheon, 1982.

Wright, Louis B. *The Cultural Life of the American Colonies 1607–1763.* New York, NY: Harper & Row, 1957.

Young, Brigadier Peter, ed. *The World Almanac of World War II.* New York, NY: World Almanac, 1981.

Zinn, Howard. *A People's History of the United States.* New York, NY: Harper & Row, 1980.

Index

Jeff Levie
Kings of Cocaine